P9-BJT-713

NEW DIRECTIONS FOR COMMUNITY COLLEGES

Arthur M. Cohen
EDITOR-IN-CHIEF

Florence B. Brawer
ASSOCIATE EDITOR

Integrating Technology on Campus: Human Sensibilities and Technical Possibilities

Kamala Anandam
Miami-Dade Community College

EDITOR

WITHDRAWN

Number 101, Spring 1998

JOSSEY-BASS PUBLISHERS
San Francisco

ERIC®
Clearinghouse for Community Colleges

INTEGRATING TECHNOLOGY ON CAMPUS: HUMAN SENSIBILITIES AND TECHNICAL POSSIBILITIES
Kamala Anandam (ed.)
New Directions for Community Colleges, no. 101
Volume XXVI, number 1
Arthur M. Cohen, Editor-in-Chief
Florence B. Brawer, Associate Editor

New Directions for Community Colleges is indexed in Current Index to Journals in Education (ERIC).

Microfilm copies of issues and articles are available in 16mm and 35mm, as well as microfiche in 105mm, through University Microfilms Inc., 300 North Zeeb Road, Ann Arbor, Michigan 48106-1346.

ISSN 0194-3081   ISBN 0-7879-4234-0

NEW DIRECTIONS FOR COMMUNITY COLLEGES is part of The Jossey-Bass Higher and Adult Education Series and is published quarterly by Jossey-Bass Inc., Publishers, 350 Sansome Street, San Francisco, California 94104-1342, in association with the ERIC Clearinghouse for Community Colleges. Periodicals postage paid at San Francisco, California, and at additional mailing offices. POSTMASTER: Send address changes to New Directions for Community Colleges, Jossey-Bass Inc., Publishers, 350 Sansome Street, San Francisco, California 94104-1342.

SUBSCRIPTIONS cost $55.00 for individuals and $98.00 for institutions, agencies, and libraries. Prices subject to change.

THE MATERIAL in this publication is based on work sponsored wholly or in part by the Office of Educational Research and Improvement, U.S. Department of Education, under contract number RI-93-00-2003. Its contents do not necessarily reflect the views of the Department or any other agency of the U.S. Government.

EDITORIAL CORRESPONDENCE should be sent to the Editor-in-Chief, Arthur M. Cohen, at the ERIC Clearinghouse for Community Colleges, University of California, 3051 Moore Hall, 405 Hilgard Avenue, Los Angeles, California 90095-1521.

Cover photograph © Rene Sheret, After Image, Los Angeles, California, 1990.

www.josseybass.com

9 7 4

CONTENTS

EDITOR'S NOTES

As early as 1970, Illich proposed that the "search for new educational funnels must be reversed into the search for their institutional inverse: educational webs which heighten the opportunity for each one to transform each moment of his living into one of learning, sharing, and caring" (1970, p. ix). Between then and now we have heard many loud pronouncements of a technology revolution that could render his proposal a reality. Has the technology revolution materialized? Is it upon us? Or is it around the corner? The much-touted paperless revolution never came. Living in America, one would think that the cellular technology revolution is upon us. But if one takes a global view and learns that two-thirds of the five billion people inhabiting this earth have never made or received a telephone call (CNN, 1997), one would not claim that that revolution is upon us. And what is around the corner is anyone's guess. Wells (1995) cites Wilbur Wright's statement, "I confess that in 1901, I said to my brother Orville that man would not fly for fifty years. . . . Ever since, I have distrusted myself and avoided all predictions" (p. 25). So should we all.

Yet, having a vision worth working toward is highly desirable if not essential (Gilbert, 1997). In educational institutions all across the world, efforts toward Illich's vision are becoming evident, although in many instances the emphasis is misplaced on technology as the end rather than the means. Interestingly enough, Illich did not mention technology in his statement but rather spoke about the processes of learning, sharing, and caring as the goal. After years of heavy investment in technology and in spite of pockets of excellence in the use of technology, educators are beginning to recognize that the focus on technology has undermined the respect for human processes that create a vision, inspire a sense of mission, and encourage a passion to pursue the vision. Sir John Daniel of the Open University writes that "technology always involves people and their social systems. So when you use technology in education, remember that processes, approaches, rules, and ways of organizing things are just as important as the devices with colored lights that we call hardware" (1997, p. 14).

The authors of the chapters in this volume, all pioneers in integrating technology in education, address the topics of organizational structures, comprehensive planning, innovative strategies, policies and procedures and, above all, collaborative approaches to achieve significant and enduring results. In Chapter One, Neff describes her college's Center for Interactive Learning, which is emphasizing the human side of the technology integration equation and the idea of a "parallel college" to overcome the traditional policies and procedures. In Chapter Two, Gellman-Danley and Teague present a case for a "unified technology center" whose members can decide on the priorities and projects for each year so that the whole college community can work together. In Chapter Three, Ehrmann articulates the "triple challenge" facing educational institutions and proposes a conceptual model for using technology, low and high, to transform the college. In Chapter Four, Bleed calls for "the biggest bang for the buck" by directing technology investment to the top twenty-five enrollment courses. In Chapter Five, Moran and Payne advocate building a human infrastructure in institutions and thus humanizing the integration of technology. In Chapter Six, Mastroni and Schwartz explain the concept of comprehensive planning and incremental implementation, which, in spite of looking like a fragmented approach, is the reality for many colleges. In Chapter Seven, I describe Project SYNERGY, a long-term collaboration among colleges to address the problems of underprepared college students that resulted in the Project SYNERGY Integrator, a tool for change. In Chapter Eight, Allison and Scott focus on faculty obligation and reasonable compensation in a technology-based educational environment and allude to the inevitable gap between planning and implementation. In Chapter Nine, Doucette describes the competition that community colleges face from for-profit content providers and suggests ways to meet those challenges.

Some common threads run through these chapters: think institutional, long-term, and holistic; focus on mainstream faculty and not just the champions of technological change; be pragmatic and adaptive; consider the human aspects of an educational revolution using technology as our greatest ally.

In 1994, Geoghegan raised a question: "Can information technology really enter the mainstream of teaching and learning?" He claimed that the barrier preventing penetration into mainstream is "less a matter of aversion to technology as it is an aversion to risk . . . and perhaps the lack of an absolutely compelling reason to buy into a new and relatively disruptive way to go about one's work" (p. 14). It is true that the hardware and software have not been reliable and stable and that the perennial desire to upgrade one or the other or both has been disruptive. That is the nature of the beast arising out of the technology race in which both vendors and educators participate. Therefore, it is all the more important, as the authors in this volume point out, to direct our attention to building the human infrastructure within which we can identify our institutional priorities, find a compelling reason to rely on technology, provide technical and educational support in a meaningful way, and thus reduce the risk and the disruption.

I hope that after reading this volume, the audience will see clearly the essence of our collective message—any endeavor of significance requires a vision, a mission, and a passion; any endeavor of significance succeeds mostly because of collaborative strategy and collective wisdom; and any technological application of significance endures if supported by an appropriate human infrastructure. I also hope that readers will explore the additional references cited in the last chapter. Finally, I urge readers to respond to the call for action that appears in Chapter Ten.

Kamala Anandam
Editor

References

CNN. "Early Morning News." July 31, 1997.
Daniel, J. S. "Why Universities Need Technology Strategies." *Change*, July/Aug. 1997, pp. 10–17.
Geoghegan, W. "Stuck at the Barricades." *AAHE Bulletin,* Sept. 1994, pp. 13–16.
Gilbert, S. "Vision Worth Working Toward." In AAHESGIT Listserv. [http://www.aahe.org]. Jan. 14, 1997.
Illich, I. *Deschooling Society.* New York: HarperCollins, 1970.
Wells, M. "Peering into the Future with Wilbur and Orville Wright." *The Futurist,* July/Aug. 1995, pp. 22–25.

KAMALA ANANDAM is associate dean of educational technologies and director of Project SYNERGY at Miami-Dade Community College and author of several articles on holistic approaches to integrating teaching and learning with technology.

The convergence of computing technology and telecommunications has become a powerful catalyst for extraordinary changes at Sinclair Community College.

Technology as a Catalyst for Reinventing an Institution

Kathryn J. Neff

In Dayton, Ohio, the year 1887 was a year of beginnings. Orville Wright enrolled in Central High School. The National Cash Register Company (NCR) hit the jackpot, selling fifty-four hundred machines after its first three years of sluggish sales. David A. Sinclair, general secretary of the Dayton YMCA, founded an evening school for men; fifty-five students signed up for courses in arithmetic and mechanical drawing at the one-room school.

One hundred and ten years later, Dayton is known internationally as the birthplace of aviation and the home of Wright Patterson Air Force Base. NCR no longer makes cash registers but continues to do business in the computing industry. David Sinclair's one-room YMCA school has grown into Sinclair Community College, where twenty thousand students enroll every term at its twenty-acre downtown campus.

During the twentieth century, Sinclair Community College transformed itself from a one-room evening school into a thriving YMCA College, an expanding Dayton Technical School, and then one of the larger community colleges in the country. Throughout this transformation, Sinclair has remained close to its roots, serving adult learners in the Dayton community as the needs of individuals and businesses evolved with the changing times. The growth has been both exciting and traumatic. Daytonians have regularly found themselves at the cutting edge of technology in the community's primary sectors of employment—aviation and defense, automotive manufacturing, and computing. In response to technological change in these dynamic areas, Sinclair has enthusiastically updated its curriculum to keep pace with the new technologies of the workplace, and over the years it has developed a culture that places unusually high value on innovation.

Yet during the first century of Sinclair's existence, the impact of technology on the institution itself—that is, its educational processes and pedagogy—was almost negligible. David Sinclair could have stepped out of his 1887 one-room school and into a 1987 classroom, picked up a piece of chalk, and finished his lecture without missing a beat. He would probably have been astonished by the diversity of a twentieth-century math class and perhaps appalled by the students' appearance (not to mention their music). But the classroom itself, the lecture-based delivery format, paper-and-pencil tests, textbooks, homework assignments, and class meeting schedules would have been completely familiar to him.

In the 1990s, however, the convergence of computing technology and telecommunications has become a powerful catalyst for revolutionary change at Sinclair. If David Sinclair were to make another short hop in his trip through time, leaping from 1987 to 1997, he would find the college involved in the process of transforming itself once again, now into a very different kind of business. If he arrived in the year 1997, David Sinclair might land in the middle of a computer lab, in front of a camera in a distance learning classroom, or somewhere in cyberspace with his virtual class on the Web. He might find himself in a multimedia studio with a team of instructors, artists, and videographers preparing interactive materials for digital distribution to remote students. David Sinclair would have loved it! Deeply committed to his personal maxim "Find the need and endeavor to meet it," he would definitely have been an "early adopter" of technology for delivering education to adult learners at their homes or places of employment, in shopping malls or public libraries. He would have been quick to see the potential of bringing consulting experts from California or Argentina or Scotland into the classroom through two-way videoconferencing or satellite downlink.

The need for lifelong learning and access to higher education has not changed in 110 years, but new technologies are providing exciting new ways to meet the need.

Find the Need and Endeavor to Meet It

Much like David Sinclair's students in 1887, the students attending Sinclair Community College in 1997 are adults with jobs and families. Their average age is over thirty-two years. Many are the first in their families to attend college. A significant number are returning to college after many years away from the classroom. Their academic backgrounds vary from high school diplomas—or General Education Diplomas (GEDs)—to advanced degrees; their goals, motivations, and learning styles are equally diverse. Considering this diversity, it has long been apparent that students at Sinclair need instructional delivery choices in addition to (or in place of) the traditional classroom lecture format. In recent years, Sinclair has responded creatively to this need, using technology to enhance access to its course offerings.

TV Sinclair. Established ten years ago, TV Sinclair is an independent study program that offers students an alternative to traditional classroom learning. Instead of attending courses in a classroom on campus, students enrolled in TV Sinclair receive course lectures and instructional materials via videocassette, audiocassette, and printed materials. Most of these courses have been developed by Sinclair faculty. Currently, over seventy different courses are available on a regular basis with more than two thousand enrollments per quarter and over seventy-five thousand enrollments annually.

Electronic College. Sinclair's Electronic College is a means for students to take courses by using computers and modems to interact with instructors. Course lectures on videotape and audiocassette are checked out for the entire quarter at no charge. Once students have listened to a lecture, they participate in interactive discussions over the World Wide Web. In addition to being able to download and print a hard copy of the lecture, students can also access all course information, including assignments and due dates, on the computer. Sinclair currently offers sixteen courses on the Web, with more to be added every quarter.

LEARNing Works. The Lifelong Education and Resource Network (LEARNing Works) program, a partnership of Sinclair Community College, Wright State University, and Greater Dayton Public Television, is a regional television network that provides interactive voice and data communication and multiple channels of educational programming. A LEARNing Works course is transmitted live from a sophisticated electronic classroom at Sinclair. Remote learners, whether they are studying in high schools, working in fire stations, or staying home in the Dayton area, interact with instructors at the Sinclair campus, using a combination of microwave video transmission and telephone communication.

The Center for Interactive Learning

Sinclair's Center for Interactive Learning (CIL) was established in 1994. The CIL's mission is to build on the programs for nontraditional course delivery already in place at Sinclair and to carry these initiatives further through the use of technology. Its goal is to promote interactive learning, with an emphasis on the assimilation of instructional technology into the curriculum and the expansion of technology-based course delivery options. To this end, the CIL functions as an incubator where faculty members redesign their curricula, investigate new learning methods, develop interactive instructional materials, and work out implementation plans to replicate and disseminate successful pilot projects.

The center, which currently occupies one multimedia lab and two classrooms, will have moved into a new building by the time this volume goes to press. In addition to providing "incubator" classrooms for pilot projects, the new CIL building will also house distance learning facilities, media production studios, employee training labs, exhibits of innovative instructional technologies, and partnership space where Sinclair faculty can work with external partners from business and industry, K–12 educators, vendors, and other organizations.

The planning of the CIL building and its operational processes has been undertaken by a CIL task force directed by Sinclair's provost and president-elect, Dr. Ned Sifferlen. The task force consists of Sinclair's four vice presidents, the director of the CIL, the dean of distance learning, three faculty members, and Sinclair's facilities manager. A consulting architect, Peter Capone, and a technology consultant, David Lehman, have guided much of the deliberations of the task force.

Since 1994, the task force has been brainstorming, constructing a vision of the CIL, and visiting high-technology sites. These sites include Silicon Graphics in Mountain View, California; Time-Warner Cable's experimental test site for interactive television in Orlando; Jones Cable in Denver; and the University of Michigan, where plans were under way at the time of the task force's visit for that school's new Media Union (an integrated technology center), which is now in operation.

The Vision of the CIL. The Center for Interactive Learning is a place where people of diverse backgrounds can see and experience the future of learning and work. In the CIL, students, faculty, and staff connect with global communities of learners to share knowledge and ideas, invent the future, and construct personal paths into that future. The CIL is simultaneously a place that empowers people through technology and a place that honors scholarship.

Above all, the Sinclair Community College Center for Interactive Learning is a place where everyone is a student. In the center, we can fearlessly try out new ways of learning and teaching, evaluate our experiments, and ponder their implications. We also aim to assimilate our best ideas into the fabric of Sinclair's academic programs and culture, and to disseminate our innovations to a regional, national, and worldwide audience.

The CIL task force has been working on the architectural design of the building and details of its construction as well as on the definition of operational processes. How will faculty and staff get involved with the CIL? What will they do while they are in the CIL? The deliberation of the task force has yielded the results described in the next section.

Pilot Projects. In 1993 Sinclair established an internal fund of $200,000 per year to fund innovative pilot projects. These grants, titled Learning Challenge Awards, are offered on a competitive basis to faculty and staff for projects that will promote interactive learning. The awards vary from about $1,000 to nearly $50,000. The funds are used primarily for faculty reassigned time, equipment, software, travel, and other project expenses. Awards are given only to teams, not to individuals. Proposals are selected for funding by a committee of faculty members that is chaired by the vice president for instruction. The projects have a two-year time limit, and the team is required to report the outcomes and impacts of the project in a final report. Nearly half of Sinclair's full-time faculty members have participated on Challenge grant teams, which have also included many staff members, administrators, and even external partners. In 1996, a portion of the Learning Challenge Awards fund was targeted specifically for projects that will be piloted in the new CIL building in fall 1998.

The selection process for these projects was somewhat different from the usual competitive bid process. Thirty faculty members were selected to participate in extensive brainstorming sessions facilitated by the technology consultant David Lehman with the objective of identifying initial pilot projects for the CIL. In these sessions, Lehman encouraged faculty members to think "out of the box," that is, beyond the constraints of the traditional classroom boundaries of time and space. The faculty members were challenged to make use of the technologies in the CIL building in innovative ways, to come up with unique delivery formats and course content. Following are a few of the initial pilot projects that emerged from the brainstorming process and have been selected for funding:

Multidisciplinary Approach to Emergency Care. Using a sophisticated human-patient simulator, this team will develop a series of instructional modules to train multidisciplinary teams of students to respond to emergency situations, provide transport for victims, and care for clients in trauma centers or emergency rooms. The project participants represent the departments of nursing, emergency medical services, respiratory care, radiological technology, fire science, and criminal justice. The human-patient simulator is a full-scale, fully interactive, lifelike simulator developed at the University of Florida.

Go Through Hell with Dante and Mitchner. Professor Gary Mitchner and colleagues will pilot a dramatic version of the course LIT 230, Great Books of the Western World. In this course, students will explore Dante's *Inferno* in a multimedia environment. Mitchner will combine the art, music, and politics of Dante's time to present the first three circles of Dante's hell. Student teams will then use the CIL facilities to create their own multimedia representations of the remaining circles.

Cyber COM 211. Sinclair's communication arts department will develop and pilot a restructured version of the course COM 211, Effective Speaking, using an extensive array of CIL technologies and facilities. The course will present core concepts to large groups, and smaller teams will plan presentations. They will use the CIL open lab facilities and classrooms to develop multimedia materials. The students enrolled in Cyber COM 211 will also be exposed to videoconferencing and Internet communication, which will prepare them for the business world of the future. COM 211 is a required course for many Sinclair programs and usually has an enrollment of about twelve hundred students per year.

Faculty Development

One of the CIL's most critical functions is professional development and training for faculty and staff in the use of instructional technologies. For over three years, the existing CIL has been conducting summer workshops and drop-in tutoring and consulting during the academic year. More than a hundred faculty members participate in the summer institute each year and attend several workshops. Most of the workshops are half-day sessions taught by early-adopter faculty members. The format is informal (blue jeans, sneakers, T-shirts), with the aim of providing a low-stress environment for technophobic faculty to try interactive technology. Faculty members are not paid to teach or attend the sessions.

In planning for professional development, the CIL has been using a model of the adoption of instructional technology developed by Stephen Gilbert, Director of Technology Projects, American Association of Higher Education. We call this "the Gilbert Model," with apologies to Stephen for taking some liberties with his work. (More accurately, it should be called a "Gilbert-Inspired Model.") This model describes the phases that faculty members and institutions progress through during the transformation to student-centered learning (Green and Gilbert, 1995).

Phase 1: Personal Productivity. Faculty usually begin working with technology using desktop computer applications. They are still lecturing but are more productive in their preparation and record-keeping.

Phase 2: Lecture Enhancement. Faculty members use technologies such as PowerPoint, graphic presentation software, to improve their lectures. They are still lecturing, but their use of presentation technologies results in more organized lectures that appeal to visual learners.

Phase 3: Interactivity. In this phase, instructors design learning activities in which the students are actively engaged. The instructors are now facilitators, lecturing only occasionally. However, the class is still structured according to the traditional paradigm, meeting at a fixed time and place for several hours each week.

Phase 4: Student-Centered Learning. In this final phase, instructors are able to provide students with many learning options beyond the classroom setting. Student-centered learning is customer-driven, designed to meet the needs of the student rather than the convenience of the institution and the faculty. The format might be a class size of one individual logging onto the Internet at 3:00 A.M. It might involve the formation of a learning community collaborating on a team project. The instructor is now a coach, facilitator, counselor, and instructional designer.

Progression Through the Phases. By description, the model may appear somewhat simplistic, implying that everyone in the institution moves at a uniform rate from one phase to the next. In reality, the institution is in all four phases at the same time, and individuals sometimes operate in multiple phases simultaneously. However, the model is useful in that it helps us track our progress over time.

According to a comprehensive survey of faculty members' use of computers and technology in 1990, approximately 44 percent of the faculty were not using computers at all, about 38 percent could be classified as being in

Phase 1, about 3 percent in Phase 2, and about 15 percent in Phase 3. Six years later, in the fall of 1996, only approximately 5 percent of the faculty were still not using technology, whereas about 46 percent were in Phase 1, 15 percent were in Phase 2, 30 percent in Phase 3, and 4 percent in Phase 4. It has taken Sinclair faculty six years to progress solidly through one phase. We expect our evolution to speed up through the phases, however. It is our experience that the first phase presents the primary barrier; as faculty members acquire some basic skills, they tend to move more rapidly into the subsequent phases.

Each of the phases in our Gilbert Model presents the institution with a unique set of challenges. During Phase 1, the primary challenge is to motivate faculty members to get involved with the transformation and dedicate the time needed to become adept with instructional technologies. As faculty members respond to this challenge and move into Phase 2, the institution is challenged to provide technical and instructional design support for their efforts. In Phase 3, the institution must address the issue of the campus information infrastructure required for interactivity through the Internet and Intranet, along with support for networked applications and groupware. Although the challenges encountered in the first three phases are daunting, they pale in comparison with the challenge that the final phase presents the institution: reengineering administrative processes and organizational structures. As we work our way through this progression at Sinclair, we are finding that the transitions through the first three phases are rather smooth, assuming that faculty members are willing to accept innovation. It is during the leap from Phase 3 to Phase 4 that we confront the organizational barriers that define the old paradigm.

Examples of Administrative Barriers

Following are some examples of organizational and administrative barriers that have been encountered at Sinclair.

Case 1. In fall 1994, Sinclair received a $5 million grant from the National Science Foundation (NSF) to establish a National Center for Excellence in Advanced Manufacturing Education (NCE/AME). The participants in this project have defined and developed a student-centered curriculum consisting of instructional modules that incorporate authentic learning experiences, contextual learning, competency-based assessment, and interdisciplinary instruction. Although the advanced manufacturing curriculum is competency-based, it was necessary to redefine the program in terms of traditional courses and credit hours so that students could receive credits that are recognized as part of a degree program and are transferable to other institutions. Delivery of the modules is also a challenge. Modules that integrate disciplines such as math and physics are designed to be taught by interdisciplinary teams. This cross-divisional team teaching has raised complicated issues in calculating faculty compensation and in reporting student enrollments from two disciplines that have different state subsidy levels (technical versus nontechnical).

Case 2. A number of faculty members at Sinclair are working with the "process learning" initiative, whose aim is to develop collaborative learning activities designed to shift the responsibility of learning to the student. In these activities students work together in teams in which individuals assume different roles to solve problems collaboratively. Many faculty members are finding that their students are traumatized by this shift; students are deeply resentful because their instructors are not lecturing. The paradigm shift to student-centered learning will not be accomplished until our students—our customers—are ready to alter their expectations of higher education and willing to become actively engaged in the learning process.

Case 3. A faculty member in the engineering and industrial technologies division is now leading a team effort to develop a student-centered drafting course, which will be piloted in the new CIL building. Students who enroll in this course will begin by taking a computer-based test to assess their knowledge of drafting. This assessment exercise will enable them to bypass portions of the course in which they are already proficient and concentrate on modules of instruction most appropriate for their personal and professional goals. As a result, the students will not waste time in class covering material that is already familiar (or irrelevant) and will be able to focus more time and energy on topics that apply to their career objectives. Although the instructional design of this course has been a significant challenge, the accompanying administrative barriers are even more formidable. Sinclair has a process in place for testing out of an entire course by taking a proficiency exam, but there is no provision for testing out of portions of a course. Will the student receive credit for the entire course? Will the student pay the full fee for the course? What about faculty payload computations? What about financial aid requirements where class attendance is mandatory?

Case 4. As a community college, Sinclair has adopted a "shamrock" model of staffing, in which the three leaves of the shamrock are represented by a core of full-time employees, a large complement of part-time faculty and staff, and judicious use of external consultants. The shamrock model clearly provides significant flexibility in responding to fluctuations in enrollments and the changing needs of the Dayton and Miami Valley community. But as our learning paradigm becomes more technological, our dependence on part-time faculty presents a new challenge. Computer literacy and skills with instructional technology are no longer merely "nice to have" but essential in most disciplines. Will part-time faculty members be required to acquire sophisticated skills so that they can teach in a distance learning environment? Will they be required to have skills in Web authoring? Or development of computer-based test banks? Will the college have resources to support them if they want to acquire and use these skills? Will they all be able to participate fully in the college's electronic dialogues? Will they be given e-mail addresses and access to all the networked personal productivity tools?

Business Not as Usual: The Parallel College

In order to identify and address the organizational challenges associated with student-centered learning, Sinclair administrators have formed a task force charged with establishing a "parallel college" that will operate in conjunction with CIL pilot projects. The parallel college will establish new procedures and policies wherever they might be needed to facilitate the adoption of new learning options. This might include faculty compensation, scheduling of space, fee structures, curriculum development processes, or any other aspect of institutional operation.

The parallel college is funded through a $200,000 grant from the NSF. This grant targets institutionwide reform in three areas: misalignment of curriculum formats with modern delivery systems, misalignment of curriculum outcomes with modern workplace requirements, and misalignment of college operating systems with modern operating systems. The parallel college team will identify obstacles and develop proposed solutions in the form of scenarios for new procedures and policies. The team will then work with Sinclair's board of trustees and the Ohio Board of Regents to implement the reforms.

Conclusion

Sinclair Community College has been serving the Dayton and Miami Valley community in Ohio for 110 years, and throughout its existence it has been expanding and continually transforming itself to meet the changing needs of individuals seeking to improve their lives through education. In recent years, Sinclair's transformation has been accelerating as a result of technological advances in computing and telecommunications. With these new technologies, Sinclair can offer unprecedented access to education and more individualized options for contextual, interactive learning. With the construction of its new Center for Interactive Learning, Sinclair is positioning itself to take a leadership role in the adoption and utilization of instructional technology through its initiatives in distance learning, curriculum development, applied research in instructional delivery, and professional development.

Reference

Green, K., and Gilbert, S. "Great Expectations: Content, Communications, Productivity, and the Role of Information Technology in Higher Education." *Change*, Mar./Apr. 1995, pp. 8–18.

KATHRYN J. NEFF *is the director of the Center for Interactive Learning at Sinclair Community College.*

*The rapid integration of technology into colleges poses a real challenge
to traditional organizational structures. This chapter describes
centralized and decentralized models, and one institution's successful
unified technology unit. Current trends are explained and
reengineering options are presented.*

Navigating the Organizational Maze: Reengineering to Advance the Technology Agenda

Barbara Gellman-Danley, Robert G. Teague

American higher education institutions are organized in rather traditional, recognizable units established to achieve specific goals. The units of this organizational structure typically include academic affairs, student affairs, and administrative affairs, all drawn along definite functional lines. But with the advent of technology integration, the demarcation between units, albeit tidy, is no longer possible. Administrative functions, once the sole purview of mainframe operations, are now widespread throughout the campus because of distributed computing and networking systems. And although academic content may belong to the instructional leaders of the college, the equipment and delivery systems may not. Consequently, the lines of demarcation between organizational units and the delineation of tasks within those units have blurred. The ubiquitous presence of new technology and its applications challenge every traditional organizational chart found in higher education.

These challenges have naturally created a tension about the administrative oversight of technology and concomitant support for its users. Perhaps until the 1980s, there was no need for technology positions in academic affairs. Administrative computing staff, and sometimes staff within the academic affairs office, handled the business operations, which were supported by mainframes and limited networking. But in the 1980s, everything changed. Suddenly, faculty and staff began to recognize the need for more "controls" and for support for classrooms, laboratories, and learning centers. The perception was then (and still is on some campuses), that the administrative computing staff simply does not understand the academic world. The controls—policies and procedures that were in place for larger systems—did not apply to new ones. Priorities were unclear. Without some organizational shifts in responsibility, many institutions found themselves struggling to move the academic technology agendas forward. Political infighting has been the inevitable and unfortunate result.

This chapter addresses the role of technology in determining organizational possibilities for colleges as well as the politics involved in attempting to integrate academic, student support, and administrative functions. The "quick fixes" adopted by institutions to keep pace with technology have only provided temporary relief from political wrangling. At Monroe Community College, the president and the board decided that the best way to advance the technology integration was to "think outside the box" of traditional organizational structure and creatively navigate the organizational maze that has arisen in the information age.

Traditional Information Technology (IT) Structures

For the purposes of this discussion, technology units include, but are not limited to, computing, networking, television production, distance learning, graphics, printing, portions of the library, equipment maintenance and repair, instructional design and support, telecommunications, computerized learning centers and labs, electronic classrooms, and the training programs that support each. A brief review of technology integration in community colleges over three decades follows.

The 1970s. In the decade of the 1970s, administrative applications of technology dominated and instructional utilization was beginning. Several trends can be identified: mainframe operations focused on administrative applications; the dominant media used in the classroom were filmstrips, 35-millimeter slides, and overhead projectors; personal computers (PCs) began to appear in offices; libraries used the Online College Library Catalogue (OCLC) for cataloguing; and distance learning was limited to telecourses and some one-way video and two-way audio television. Generally, academic and administrative functions were separate.

The 1980s. Several changes took place in the 1980s, marking a steady growth of technology available to users. Library services, which were on-line, became distributed to users and were no longer the sole purview of librarians; mainframe applications continued to handle administrative systems but PCs were used for both business and academic applications by faculty, staff, and students; local area networks (LANs) grew in departments; more robust telecommunications systems were adopted; distance learning expanded to include interactive video; and computerized labs and learning centers appeared as academic support services. Training was becoming increasingly necessary, and staffing needs grew from more specialized personnel to positions requiring a variety of skills to serve various academic units.

The 1990s. The changes during the 1990s to date have been so accelerated that they mark the onset of what may be called "the information revolution" on campuses. Community colleges have been challenged to look at their organizational structures and determine whether the traditional units even fit any more. In many cases, they do not.

Libraries have become fully automated and more dependent on technology; PCs have become standard office equipment; students come to colleges expecting both equipment and software availability; networking has infused new communications systems in colleges and created ways for departments to get connected to both administrative and academic programs; distance learning has become a common term representing a wide range of delivery systems, including interactive video and audio, and asynchronous learning through computers; the Internet and the World Wide Web offer alternate delivery modes; and students expect on-line access to registration, grades, and catalogues.

Organizationally, the challenge has been formidable. There are no longer distinct lines drawn between the administrative and academic service units. In some cases, skilled employees have been difficult to recruit and retain, a continuing problem. Too often, colleges have found their staff educated in the 1970s but needing skills for the 1990s. Presidents have been driven to examine the need for information technology reengineering.

The Impact of Technology on Institutions. Because of the impact of technology, several trends among colleges—regardless of their size, age, or location—have surfaced: there is a perception that the administrative computing area receives more funds and more staff than the academic side; many believe that long-term employees hired in the early years of college development do not have the skills to maintain new systems; faculty often cite the loss of academic freedom with respect to technology applications and most do not easily accept that administrative staff understand the implications of this autonomy; technology leaders and support staff identify the need for standardization while the users find standardization too controlling; board members, chancellors, and presidents are interested in controlling the escalating costs of technology and turn toward reengineering and downsizing as the way to maximize the investment; and each side of the organization puts increasing importance on disproving the other's credibility in managing technology. These concerns, whether real or imagined, are very typical across the country.

In some cases, the leadership is simply trying to sift through the chaos and find new rules of operation. In others, the relationships are either unclear or, sometimes, hostile. Hammer (Hammer and Champy, 1993) noted that "merely throwing computers at an existing business problem does not cause it to be reengineered. In fact, the misuse of technology can block reengineering altogether by reinforcing old ways of thinking and old behavior patterns" (p. 83). Practices in higher education reflect that concern.

Instructional Telecommunications Council Survey. Realizing that the 1990s have brought forth a variety of challenges to the existing organizational structures, the authors conducted a national survey in 1996 to find out how colleges organized themselves in order to facilitate the integration of technology (Gellman-Danley, 1993). The survey consisted of twenty-nine short-answer or multiple-choice questions and was administered to the four hundred members of the Instructional Telecommunications Council (ITC) of the American Association of Community Colleges.

These institutions varied widely in size from 443 to approximately 125,000 full-time students; the average size was 4,784 full-time and 5,480 part-time students, with 147 full-time faculty. The institutions' administrative structure was flatter than anticipated. The number of direct reports to the president (or chancellor) averaged 7.67. The average number of vice presidents and vice chancellors was 1.86; titles of executive director, director, and dean made up the other remaining 6 direct reports to the president.

The heart of the survey concerned IT organization. Although about 70 percent of both the large and the small institutions did not have a unified IT organization, it was gaining in popularity, as mentioned by 41 percent of the institutions. Among those that had an IT organization, most had existed for 4.8 years.

Generally, there was a chief information officer (CIO) or equivalent leading the IT organization (reported by 74 percent of the respondents). The CIO reported directly to the president or chancellor 48 percent of the time, to the academic vice president 10 percent of the time, and to the administrative vice president 33 percent of the time. The remaining 9 percent of CIOs did not respond to the question about reporting policy.

Equipment purchases were budgeted at the department level most often (73 percent of survey respondents reported this). However, maintenance and upgrading were most often budgeted at the vice presidential or institutional level (44 percent and 45 percent, respectively). Unfortunately, 10 percent of institutions reported that they did not budget for maintenance and upgrading at all.

The survey reinforced our belief that there is interest in moving toward some form of consolidated IT organization, although that transformation has been slow. The circumstances were different at each institution, and many indicated the need to find a proper organizational structure for technology within the confines of existing staff, budget, and political culture.

The Unified IT Organization. It is very important to note that every institution is unique and that many factors influence organizational structures. Relevant factors include the people who currently hold the various positions, the placement of budgetary responsibility, leadership's commitment to technology at various levels, the college's readiness for change, communication channels already in place, and a variety of other issues that affect the final decision. Therefore, no one structure is appropriate for all colleges.

The stand-alone IT organization will work if the unit is neutral, fair, provides leadership rather than control, acts toward consensus building, takes responsibility for providing service and training, remains current, offers strong communication channels, and willingly shares budgetary resources across the various units and technologies. It will not succeed if it mirrors traditional ways of operating, simply placed within a new structure. The unit will not succeed, for example, if leaders hire support staff who are single-task oriented or unwilling to work as part of a team. That approach reflects former, less useful models.

Whether they are placed within an existing unit or are stand-alone, unified IT organizations must have the ear of the chief executive officer. For that reason alone, many colleges prefer to place the unified IT under a chief information officer or vice president or vice chancellor. With the increased presence of technology at the colleges and in the communities they serve, it is advisable to assure that the person in charge remains very aware of all the implications of the rapidly changing environment. Many colleges believe this information and advocacy requires a direct reporting structure.

The Monroe Community College Experience

Monroe Community College (MCC) was opened in 1961 as part of the State University of New York (SUNY) system of community colleges to provide technical, paraprofessional, and university-transferable education. It is one of thirty community colleges in the state and is a member of the League for Innovation in the Community College. At its two campuses, MCC enrolls more than fourteen thousand full- and part-time students for accredited courses each semester; several thousand more take nonaccredited courses through the college's corporate training and community education programs. MCC is unionized and has a president as chief executive officer of the college. It is recognized for its innovative applications of technology, and its overarching mission is student success.

In 1994, Monroe Community College began to make the transition toward a stand-alone IT organization. Outside consultants recommended that a chief information officer at the vice presidential level be appointed who would report to the president. Internally, it became increasingly clear that academic and administrative computing needed better linkages.

On encouragement of the board of trustees and the president, a total reengineering was undertaken, resulting in the formation of the Educational Technology Services division in fall 1995. This organizational model includes the college libraries; all computing, networking, telecommunications, and instructional support (graphics, video); distance learning; printing; equipment repair and maintenance; technology training; a help desk; "smart classroom" support; and a large computerized learning center. Importantly, the terms *academic* and *administrative* were removed from computing, and the term *educational* was selected to position the unit as placing a priority on academics while also providing a wide range of administrative services. The terminology helps with the perceptions described in earlier sections.

The Development of Educational Technology Services. The transition to this unified organization passed through several stages. First, a "neutral" vice president (student affairs) with technological acumen headed up a committee that brought together the academic and administrative leaders of technology, who were then reporting to the vice presidents of academic affairs and administrative affairs, respectively. After a few years of successfully planning projects, the committee felt the need for a more formal organizational structure under the leadership of a new vice president who would dedicate time primarily to technology-related issues.

On the departure of one of the leaders in administrative computing, the unit was moved under an existing vice president, then in charge of institutional advancement, a person with over twenty years of experience in distance learning and technology. Throughout that year, extensive college input was received on the entire college's reorganization. The result was the formation of the Educational Technology Services division in 1995, headed by the already-mentioned vice president. Institutional advancement then moved directly under the president's office. The mission of this new unit is the following: Educational Technology Services combines the college's information, communication, and technology resources into one unit with a commitment to facilitate teaching/learning processes at MCC through the implementation, advancement, and support of technology.

The Benefits of a Unified Technology Organization. This model offered the benefit of an expanded knowledge base, which reflects the collective wisdom of staff formerly working separately. The model also resulted in much better support for a variety of services, through teams that reflected the collective technical expertise of individual staff who previously worked separately. There is an expanded awareness of the roles of all staff, and a clarification of responsibilities. Training is centralized, as is the help desk, so users do not have to contact several different departments for assistance.

However, the greatest contributor to the success of the reengineering has been planning. In its second year in operation, the Educational Technology Services team developed a comprehensive technology plan for the college, with input from over 350 faculty and staff. The result is a very clear vision for the future, including cost-benefit analyses for every project suggested for the next few years. This planning process lasted nearly one year and included an external environmental analysis, a comprehensive review of existing technologies at the college, an internal analysis, sixty recommended projects, five new policies, and detailed topographies of the entire college showing the location and applications of technology. The following are examples of projects:

Virtual campus for offices: A $160,000 investment will provide a common set of tools and programs on every networked administrative/office computer on campus. It will provide software, virus protection, and so on, in ways that greatly increase services and reduce staff time needed for support, thereby increasing PC reliability.

Student information access via the World Wide Web. This is a project to provide an interface between the in-house student information system on the mainframe and the college's Web site. This facility allows the students to interact with the college's system from remote locations.

Security for Internet and Intranet configurations within the college. Security is critical to maintaining the integrity of data and to safeguard the system from viruses. The policies relate to mandated virus protection and virus protection training.

The board of trustees endorsed the plan, and the team now has a road map for its travels down the information highway. Other benefits include a sharing of resources across academic and administrative units, a coordinated instructional design team, extensive internal grants, external partnering (for example, the school became a Lotus Business Partner, enabling the college to be a certified trainer in return for complimentary or discounted software), revision and upgrading of positions to meet the needs of the 1990s, and an end to the infighting and political obstacles that once detracted from the success of technology integration.

Communication is this division's best asset. The president is very supportive of the change, and by placing a vice president for educational technology within his organization he gave a strong signal of his own commitment to the agenda. The issues of staffing shortages and resource management persist, but the team finds the unified approach effective in meeting these challenges.

Other institutions have embraced the planning model and followed a detailed workbook that MCC created on how to develop a comprehensive technology planning initiative through teamwork. This is one among the many new models available to community colleges. Warren Bennis writes of "great groups" in his recent book *Organizing Genius: The Secrets of Creative Collaboration* (Bennis and Biederman, 1997). The Educational Technology Services team, although it does not perceive itself in the same category as Bennis's examples, nevertheless has grown to believe so deeply in its mission that it fits the description of great groups. These groups find a real purpose in which to believe; they have "fire in their eyes" and an enthusiasm for a shared goal. Hierarchy is much less important than teamwork and innovation. At least at this moment in time, the unified IT model at MCC has these attributes.

Assessing Your Institution's IT Organizational Structure

The success of one institution may provide a model for others. Yet, as indicated earlier, each college is so complex and unique that individual assessments are necessary. The following paragraphs outline a ten-step process that will assist you in determining the appropriate paths for reengineering and revamping your organizational structure.

Step One: Assess Institutional Readiness for Technology. Organizational structure must follow the institution's readiness for technology. Clearly, it makes no sense for a college that is not planning to embrace a new technology agenda to be concerned with changing its organizational structure. However, institutions planning to compete in an increasingly technology-rich educational environment likely will have a paramount need to articulate the organizational structure and communication channels. Therefore, the first step is to identify the college's technological acumen, readiness to move forward, knowledge and skills to do so, and general directions for the future. This step may be very time consuming if there is no technology plan in place; if one exists it can provide helpful directives on the strengths and weaknesses within the current climate. Be sure to include representation of all groups of users. If possible, take time off from work—go together on a retreat, for example—to accomplish this first step.

Step Two: Identify Technology Presence Within the College. Begin by defining technology and what it means for your own institution. Think beyond the immediate situation to allow for the inclusion of future technologies. Within this definition, list all the "pockets" of technology present within the college. There are official institutional units responsible for technology and others where the presence is so strong that an unofficial unit of technology leadership may be forming. Consider applications, such as word processing, and identify the organizational oversight of this task if one exists. The prevalent unit will vary greatly among colleges. Identifying where technology is managed may be very enlightening. Often, institutions require a series of discussions to agree upon the areas where technology is most prevalent.

Step Three: Identify Technology Leadership. There are two types of technology leadership at a college—official and unofficial. The first type has authority due to position; the second is in most cases a technology-literate user recognized for integrating new methods of teaching and administration into existing practices. It is important to identify each in order to establish the placement of technology decision making and influence at the college. It is often the "rising stars" among faculty, for instance, who eventually receive release time to develop technology-based programs.

Step Four: Articulate the College's Mission and Technology Goals. In order to examine the organizational structure thoroughly, planners must study the institutional mission, any existing technology plans, and the ways in which the official units meet prescribed needs. If the unofficial leaders are carrying out the majority of tasks, this may indicate that some reengineering is needed. Many institutions have plans that are implemented; others write elaborate plans that never see the light of day. Study the relationship between the plan and the planners, the technology goals and the technology leadership, and determine if the college is best positioned organizationally to meet the goals and vision for the future.

Step Five: Evaluate Current Organizational Structure. At this point the strengths and weaknesses of the current structure may be examined. One institution in our survey noted that elaborate plans were available but there was no leadership to assure implementation. Another found that the official leadership did not understand the goals set forth by faculty, and therefore, it was unlikely the plan would ever be realized. Identify the strengths and weaknesses of the current structure to help you hone in on organizational voids that require a new way of thinking and doing business.

Step Six: Review the Source of Weaknesses. There will be times when the current staff does not provide adequate leadership for technology advancement. This may be a result of the staff members' own limitations, their knowledge, experience, and educational background. However, deeper problems are found at many colleges. Sometimes the official leadership is not willing to expand to new systems and programs or places too much emphasis on certain applications. In some instances, technology leaders may have weaknesses in communication that create more disharmony in the organization than is healthy. Faculty may also demonstrate a bias against administrative technology tasks. One college in our survey noted that the faculty continually denied the need for a mainframe computer despite extensive documentation that one was needed. Another explained that distributed computing was acceptable, but only if administrative computing controlled the systems. In neither case was there an indication of the flexibility needed for constructive change. Not surprisingly, many presidents had to serve as mediators in these types of disputes.

The most important goal at this stage is to determine if the differences are based on issues or people, that is, on actual practices or on perceptions. Both may imply the need for organizational reengineering. And in certain cases, there will be a need to change staffing.

Step Seven: Determine Opportunities and Options for Change.

Gains and Losses. There will be opportunities and options for organizational change. Each college should list the gains and losses associated with any change. For example, not selecting a unified technology organization may represent more gains than losses at some colleges, but it may have the reverse effect at others. One of the concerns that should be addressed is the political fallout that will be associated with each choice. It is important to note that certain decisions may be appropriate for the present time but require change in the future.

Staffing Implications. Changes may imply shifts in staffing. One myth that many colleges face is that an organizational change toward a unified technology department will automatically balance out the staff expertise. But that is not true: staff trained in the 1970s and 1980s on mainframe programming will not rapidly become distributed networking experts. The learning curves are often greater than the time the administration is willing to provide. Reason should prevail in these circumstances, with training and time for learning available to any staff expected to take on significantly different duties.

This is not to say that staff will not be able to change duties. In fact, technology support staff have a formidable challenge; they must constantly seek training and remain ahead of the curve in a rapidly changing environment. Unified organizations, or those with strong communication across divisions, find that the collaborative wisdom of support staff offers a greater opportunity to advance the technology initiatives of the college. In the ideal scenario, all the technology leaders meet on a regular basis to plan projects, systems, policies, and applications. One example often cited is the planning of new buildings. Similarly, all technology staff need to be included at the onset of this planning process or the result will be weakened solutions for wiring, networking, and general installation.

Budget Implications. Organizational shifts will have an impact on funding resources too. The impetus behind many reorganizations is funding, an attempt to pool resources and save money. It is helpful to ascertain the actual intention, as it relates to budget, of any changes in the organizational structure. List all the expectations, perceived or real, for each option and determine the actual budget implications of each option as well. For example, a split organization may not cost any more money but it will also not save any resources. A unified organization will only save resources if certain positions are blended or eliminated. In both options, be certain the real cost savings are studied before any promises are made. Again, take the example of building a new facility; too often, the structure is planned without the complete and early input of all technology specialists. It is much more expensive to fix a problem than to avoid it by good planning.

Step Eight: Establish the Process for Change Within the College. The reengineering process should be set within the existing approval processes for the institution. Change always carries with it a mix of enthusiasm and anxiety. Technology brings about the same reactions, so it is prudent not to step outside the approval parameters in this instance. This step requires identifying the approval processes, with special recognition of those individuals who will support and oppose the proposed solution. Inevitably, politics will come into play; leadership needs to be certain that the right players are kept appraised throughout the process.

Step Nine: Recommend a Plan of Action. If the college community decides to proceed with a reorganization, then it will need an action plan for implementation. This plan should include a detailed list of all the steps that will be taken, the impact on employees, and the outcomes expected. It may be helpful to bring in a team-building expert, or to find other ways to attend to the early needs of the new group.

Step Ten: Evaluate. Build in a plan to evaluate the process and the results. Find methods to communicate progress to the college community, through newsletters or bulletin boards, for example. Pay close attention to supporters and detractors within the organization. Evaluation may lead to other changes; just as technology is not static, neither are the employees carrying out its agenda.

Conclusion

The success of Monroe Community College indicates a good match between strategic technology planning and strategically placed leadership within the organization. This arrangement, although very functional, may not be needed in five to ten years. It is possible that technology will become salient enough to assure its position in the future of American higher education without concern for its organizational placement. The main point that the authors wish to leave readers with is that technology acquisition is easy; cultural and organizational shifts to make it successful may not be as smooth (Hammer and Champy, 1993). Proper planning and detailed study are needed at every college in order to guarantee the best possible outcomes for all involved and ultimately for the most important customer—the student.

References

Bennis, W., and Biederman, P. W. *Organizing Creative Genius: The Secrets of Creative Collaboration.* Reading, Mass.: Addison-Wesley, 1997.

Gellman-Danley, B. "Community College Organizational Structure: Informational/Instructional Technologies." A study of the members of the Instructional Telecommunications Council, Nov. 1993.

Hammer, M., and Champy, J. *Reengineering the Corporation: A Manifesto for Business Revolution.* New York: HarperCollins, 1993.

BARBARA GELLMAN-DANLEY is vice president, Educational Technology Services, Monroe Community College.

ROBERT G. TEAGUE is director, Educational Technology Services, Monroe Community College.

Many institutions are searching for a unifying vision to guide their investments to support teaching and learning technology. Some hear the insistent calls for innovations that foster "distance learning" and "learning anytime, anywhere for anyone" and wonder if their campuses even have a future. This chapter presents a conceptual model for integrating technology, both high and low, in a way that supports a transformation of teaching and learning.

Using Technology to Transform the College

Stephen C. Ehrmann

The search for a usable vision of the future is one reason why so many two- and four-year institutions are organizing teaching, learning, and technology roundtables (Gilbert, 1997) to discuss individual and institutional visions. Roundtables are usually internal advisory and coordinating bodies that bring together educational and technology leaders, including faculty leaders who are not techno-zealots, and students. This chapter describes a common vision of these institutions' future that is emerging (including a vision for distance education) and identifies the pressing policy questions facing educational leaders.

The first element of the emerging common vision of teaching, learning, and technology has to do with motive. On one end of the motivational spectrum, institutions are changing because they believe they have no choice. Today's workplace requires new intellectual skills because of the digital technologies on which it increasingly depends—for example, modern statistical techniques, computer-based music composition, and geographic information systems. In order to learn these skills, students must use the same or similar technologies during their education, that is, they must learn by doing.

At the other end of the spectrum, other pressing teaching and learning needs also compel educators and legislators to see as essential the use of computers, video, and telecommunications in the rebuilding of their educational offerings. The following are some of those needs:

- To widen and enrich educational access for a variety of currently underserved groups, such as working adults, the homebound (including homemakers), the handicapped, and others
- To draw on and share a wider range of intellectual resources than institutions can afford to acquire and maintain locally

New Directions for Community Colleges, no. 101, Spring 1998 © Jossey-Bass Publishers

- To implement teaching techniques that are far more feasible with the help of technology (for example, computer- and video-based airplane simulators to train pilots)

Many of these needs can be summed up as a triple challenge (Ehrmann, 1996a) that educators face in one form or another. The triple challenge is to extend access and increase the fairness of access to learning; to enrich and update what students are taught; and to control the costs for students to learn.

The Technology Tower

Institutions under these pressures are gradually rethinking their conceptual model and practices for using technology. To discuss this common vision, it is useful to use a conceptual model: a technology tower, a structure with a basement and three stories, each resting on the floor below it.

The Basement. The basement of every technology tower is a foundation of well-established technologies and the infrastructure for their use; for example, audiovisual materials, libraries, textbooks, and tutorial labs. These technologies have been around for a long time and are reliable and familiar enough that they can be used almost without any training. The buildings and facilities that house these materials are part of this foundation as well.

The First Floor. The first floor is made up of technology support for four basic dimensions of learning (Ehrmann, 1990; Ehrmann, 1996b), each made possible by the technologies in the basement.

Directed instruction. Traditional technologies in the basement that support the first-floor teaching and learning function include lecture halls and textbooks.

Learning by doing. Traditional technologies in the basement for supporting this first-floor activity include the chemistry laboratory, typewriters, the library, the internship office—all the "hardware" and "software" used in apprentice-style activities as learners acquire skills by practicing them.

Real-time conversation. Traditional technologies that support this dimension of learning include seminar facilities, faculty offices, and the campus itself. They promote both formal and informal meetings.

Time-delayed exchange. This kind of conversation, such as homework exchange, unfolds over time at a far slower and more thoughtful pace than that of a rapid-fire seminar talk. The discussion begins with the formulation of an assignment, continues when the assignment is handed in, and often ends with a grade.

The Second Floor. The second floor of the technology tower houses enhancements to teaching and learning practices that are made possible by the four types of learning support available on the first floor. Building on the basement and first-floor amenities, many institutions are reconstructing the second floor of the technology tower to include support for at least three improvements in their teaching and learning practices and associated services:

Adding content. They add content that requires student use of computers, video, or telecommunications (for example, approaches to statistics or political science that require statistical software and off-campus databases or graphic arts content created with computers and associated printers).

Creating services and structures. They create services and structures that help extend access to students who work and others who find traditional class schedule hours to be difficult or impossible to use fully (these services include, for example, on-line library catalogues, on-line registration, Internet access for staff and students).

Implementing the "Seven Principles of Good Practice in Undergraduate Education." They are implementing Chickering and Gamson's principles (Chickering and Gamson, 1987; Chickering and Ehrmann, 1996) more fully. The seven principles are active learning (that is, project-based learning), collaborative learning and other forms of student-student interaction, student-faculty interaction, rich and rapid feedback, time on task, high expectations, and respect for varied talents and learning styles.

The Third Floor. The third floor of the metaphorical technology tower represents the large-scale structures of education. Until recently there were two basic ways to think about education for adults: campusbound programs and distance teaching programs. Now each of those concepts is undergoing profound changes while the system that includes them both is becoming larger and more complex, as shown in Table 3.1.

We are seeing the emergence of campus-based education (not just campusbound education) and distributed learning (not just distance teaching) and, with these two, the creation of larger-scale structures in higher education. These trends not only challenge an institution's traditional mode of operations but also offer it unprecedented opportunities to transform itself.

The campusbound paradigm assumes that the only resources of value are those found within the walls of an educational institution and that education happens only when the learner is on-site. In contrast, the campus-based paradigm assumes that some of the resources and some of the learning are off-site. In other words, the campus is an important part of, but only a part of, the learning environment.

Earlier distance teaching programs relied mainly on directed instruction often provided by mass media, for example, textbooks, television and radio broadcasts, videocassettes and audiocassettes. The other three forms of learner support—learning by doing, real-time conversation, and time-delayed exchange—could only be supported to a modest extent. In contrast, the distributed learning paradigm assumes that each learner and educator is within physical or electronic reach of substantial bodies of resources, including other educators and learners. Directed instruction is not dominant in this paradigm, and the idea of a broadcasting hub is not as central to the program as it was earlier.

A third set of top-floor challenges to institutional leadership relates to the scale of the enterprise. One of the most obvious issues of scale in distributed

Table 3.1. The Four Dimensions of Learning Support

Third Floor: Large-scale structures	Campus-based (evolving from campusbound) program. Campusbound and distributed learning programs share much of the same basement, first, and second floors.		Distributed learning programs (evolving from distance teaching). Distributed learning and campusbound programs share much of the same basement, first, and second floors.	
Second Floor: Improvements in practice enabled by the new dimensions of support	1. Content that requires student use of information technology (for example, modern statistics) 2. Structures that increase access (for example, on-line library services and counseling) 3. Better implementation of the Seven Principles of Good Practice in Undergraduate Education, for example, active (project-based) learning, collaborative learning, student-faculty interaction, rich and rapid feedback, more time on task, and so on			
First Floor: Four dimensions of support for learning	Real-time conversation (for example, seminars, brainstorming)	Time-delayed exchange (for example, homework exchange, on-line seminars)	Learning by doing, using the tools and resources of the field	Directed instruction (explanation of facts, ideas, skills, and so on)
Basement: Technologies for each of the four dimensions that progress incrementally	Traditional, for example, seminar rooms, campus to foster easy meetings. Today, also phone, audioconferencing, "chat rooms" on Internet.	Traditional, for example, campus, postal service. Today, also electronic mail, computer conferencing, fax machines.	Traditional, for example, pen, research library, laboratories, studios. Today, also word processing, statistical packages, databases, on-line library.	Traditional, for example, lecture hall, textbook. Today, also video of lecture, presentation software, computer tutorial, simulator, Web-based instructional materials.

learning arises from a simple question: "How are distant learners and distant providers supposed to find each other and work together successfully?" Many regions are beginning to create new organizations whose role is to mediate between distant learners and large numbers of distant providers of education. These organizations may be seen as the infrastructure for integrated access (Ehrmann, 1996a). Examples in the United States include the National Technological University, Education Network of Maine, Oregon EdNet, JEC College Connection (formerly known as Mind Extension University), and the proposed Western Governors University.

Supporting the Rebuilding of the Technology Tower

Obviously, rebuilding a technology tower while living and working in it costs money and causes confusion and frustration. We note briefly that rebuilding this new technology tower encompasses some special needs of its own in addition to some of the more conventional physical needs. Three of those special needs are staff and program development, coordination and collaboration, and better information for decision making.

Staff and Program Development. Better means to support and reward relatively fast-paced program and staff development are needed. Many elements of the job world are on a "digital treadmill." Rapid improvements and changes in technology require these technology-dependent fields to make rapid and sometimes unpredictable changes in the nature of their work and in the nature of their thinking. New fields pop into existence frequently and they too must be served. Thus, the faculty members, departments, and institutions serving these fast-changing job markets must change rapidly too. That takes money and rewards to support staff members and departments that take risks. It seems apparent that institutions need to take some unusual steps internally while also collaborating with one another. The INnovative Programs Using Technology (INPUT) awards program in mathematics is one example of interinstitutional sharing of ideas for rethinking courses. Run by Professor Susan Lenker of Central Michigan University with funding from the Annenberg/CPB Project and the National Science Foundation, INPUT sought mathematics courses that had been restructured in ways made possible by graphing calculators, computers, and other forms of information technologies. Suffolk Community College (New York) led the team that won the national prize for rethinking an algebra course. INPUT distributes a handbook and video designed to help other faculty and institutions profit from the experience of these pioneering programs.

Coordination and Collaboration. In some institutions, the people who share responsibility for guiding the use of technology for teaching and learning do not even know one another. It is not uncommon to observe disjointed efforts going in different directions in the same institution. Information technology requires collaboration from some unusual "bedfellows," including faculty members who are zealous about technology, faculty members with little use for technology, distance learning advocates, librarians, academic computing specialists, the bookstore personnel, the provost, the chief financial officer, and so on.

The American Association for Higher Education has been helping colleges and universities organize teaching, learning, and technology roundtables. At this writing approximately three hundred such roundtables have begun work in various universities. Roundtables bring together this disparate group of individuals to work on diverse problems, such as the support service crisis, improvement of student writing using technology, redesign of distance learning programs, and the financing of new information technologies (Gilbert, 1997).

Better Information for Decision Making. Institutions desperately need better information in order to make decisions regarding investment in technology to enhance teaching and learning. In the not-so-distant past, educational institutions changed rather slowly and deliberately. Truly novel change was unusual, which made it relatively easy to anticipate the consequences of one's actions. Today, educators need to step into the dark more often than not. Ordinarily, it is almost impossible to tell whether the kinds of anticipated changes are happening, even when they are happening on a large scale. Is an institution's investment in technology enabling its curriculum to become more up to date? Is it helping the institution to implement Chickering and Gamson's seven principles of good practice? How can one tell when answers are hidden behind hundreds of classroom walls and in the myriad places where students do homework? Because the evidence of even dramatic success or failure is likely to be subtle and because so much is at stake, educators need to spend more of their time and resources using surveys and other forms of inquiry to detect what's going on inside and outside those classroom walls. The Flashlight Project at the American Association for Higher Education is developing survey item banks and other evaluative tools that can be used to gauge progress and problems (Ehrmann, 1997).

Policy Issues for Decision Makers

As educational leaders engage in rebuilding and renovating their technology tower, it will be prudent to consider certain policy issues for the benefit of their own institutions as well as for the whole educational community.

Five Questions. Should the institution make it a general rule to invest only in technologies that are likely to be stable over long periods of time as opposed to newer and riskier technologies?

Should the institution invest in a large range of technologies or should it specialize in certain ones? Each technology has its own requirements for maintenance, training, support, and replacement.

Should the institution invest in technology to transform a few courses of study? Focusing resources to transform one or two courses of study is a far greater intellectual, political, and financial challenge than spreading resources thin so that every department gets a little.

Should the institution redirect some of its resources to improve organizational structure and operational procedures to maintain the coherence of academic programs at a time when its resources, teachers, and students are all becoming more geographically scattered and working on different time schedules?

Should the institution contribute its fair share to the networked "commons" of intellectual resources? The whole idea of distributed learning may stand or fall on the issue of whether institutions contribute to the commons or just take from it.

Wise Investment. All but the last policy issue direct attention to the question of wise investment of scarce dollars. Each institution needs to discuss these issues, taking into consideration its own vision and circumstances. The last policy issue of contributing to the commons of intellectual resources refers to the moral obligation of all institutions to add to the resources that are needed to furnish the technology tower.

References

Chickering, A., and Ehrmann, S. C. "Implementing the Seven Principles: Technology as Lever." *AAHE Bulletin,* Oct. 1996, pp. 3–6. [Also available at http://www.aahe.org/technology/ehrmann.htm.]

Chickering, A., and Gamson, Z. "Seven Principles of Good Practice in Undergraduate Education." *AAHE Bulletin,* Mar. 1987, pp. 3–7.

Ehrmann, S. C. "Reaching Students, Reaching Resources: Using Technology to Open the College." *Academic Computing,* 1990, 4 (7), 10–14, 32–34.

Ehrmann, S. C. *Information Technology and the Future of Post-Secondary Education.* Paris and Washington, D.C.: Organization for Economic Cooperation and Development, 1996a.

Ehrmann, S. C. *Adult Learning in a New Technological Era.* Paris and Washington, D.C.: Organization for Economic Cooperation and Development, 1996b. (ED 408 442)

Ehrmann, S. C. "The Flashlight Project: Spotting an Elephant in the Dark." [http://www.aahe.org/technology/elephant.htm]. Nov. 1997.

Gilbert, S. W. "Levers for Change." *TLTR Workbook.* Washington, D.C.: American Association for Higher Education, 1997.

STEPHEN C. EHRMANN is director of the Flashlight Project at the American Association of Higher Education.

This chapter proposes a practical approach to determining where investments in technology should be made. Research shows that nearly 50 percent of community college students enroll in only the top twenty-five courses. These courses are the target for increasing access and flexibility and for reducing costs—for getting the "biggest bang for the buck."

Learner-Centered Strategy for Investments in Technology in Community Colleges

Ronald D. Bleed

Just before IBM introduced its revolutionary new 360 mainframe computer in 1964, only large corporations used a computer and only five companies made them (Mobley and McKeown, 1989). The year 1964 is also the approximate time when states greatly expanded the number of community colleges through legislation and permissive funding sources. Since then, the number of computers has risen to the millions as has the number of community college students. Although both industries experienced explosive growth during the same time frame, community colleges have not been large consumers of computers compared to businesses or other institutions of higher education. In other words, growing up together did not make for a good relationship. The commitment and ability of community colleges to invest in technology vary considerably. The Maricopa Community Colleges are at the high end of the scale in terms of technology commitments. Most other community colleges have not had enough resources to make such big investments in computing. In spite of the investments, the computer revolution has not dramatically changed the way business is conducted in education as it has in other industries.

When large or small expenditures occur and outcomes are not clear, a debate usually emerges as to the merits of those technology investments. Many faculty members question the value and the cost benefits of spending huge sums of money on computers. Calls for research or evidence of the effectiveness of technology in the teaching and learning process continue. At the same time, however, legislators and tax-watch groups demand greater productivity in higher education. Respected management "gurus" like Peter

Drucker predict that higher education will follow the path already taken by health care, with a major restructuring caused by escalating costs. Many people in education hope that technology can provide the infrastructure that brings more effectiveness in costs and learning.

Massy and Zemsky (1996) introduce us to the current state of technology and its potential with these comments: "Not that innovation is lacking on the micro scale. Examples of new technology applications abound. Most institutions have made major investments in the new technologies, distributing computing capacity across their campuses, linking faculty with students as well as with one another, and generally providing the necessary information technology (IT) infrastructure that is a precondition to faculty involvement. What is missing, however, is any overarching sense of purpose along with any practical sense of what the shape and consequences of successful innovations might look like" (p. 1).

Despite high costs and other concerns, technology has gained a foothold in community colleges. Computerized systems assist in the management of the institution. Community colleges have invested in expensive software systems for student information systems, human resources systems, and financial systems. Several generations of mainframe hardware have been installed. Almost everybody is on-line.

Curricula where technology is the object of instruction are very popular. Probably most enrollment increases in community colleges over the past decade can be attributed to popular personal computer courses on such subjects as word processing, spreadsheets, and information access. Other disciplines use technology for presentations, additional learning modules, communication between faculty and students, Internet access, and multimedia demonstrations. In addition, students now access large amounts of digitized information resources in libraries.

These advances have come at the cost of a large financial trade-off for community colleges. Leadership continually asks hard questions and looks for strategic directions of where to invest scarce dollars. If technology is now inevitable, where should the dollars go to feed its voracious appetite? The human support for technology is even more scarce than dollars. Where should these "people resources" be allocated? This chapter proposes a strategy to identify an overarching sense of purpose for technology investments in community colleges. It identifies commonly used strategies for perspective purposes and then advocates one of a very practical sense.

Commonly Used Technology Investment Strategies

In order to answer the strategy questions, community colleges commonly use one of eleven approaches, sometimes in combination.

Build It and They Will Come. This strategy generally involves the building of computer labs in departments, libraries, or large areas, such as high-tech centers. The procurement of the technology precedes much of the software development. Because of funding cycles, purchasing regulations, and special "pots" of money, it has often been easier for community colleges to buy equipment than any of the other components of technology. A current version of this strategy is to construct the network first.

Reward the Heat Seekers. Every faculty group includes natural innovators; these people generally represent about 10 percent of the entire group. These are the people who are very excited about computers and doing things differently. They would innovate even without support, but administration often rewards these people with support in the form of release time, extra compensation, travel, conference presentations, or new equipment. These individuals' ideas and directions for the application of technology become the college's answer to technology planning.

Let External Funds Drive Our Projects. Because of limited internal funding sources, colleges often use the long-standing tradition of seeking grants to fund their technology projects. Accountability requires that the projects have specific outputs, but whether those outputs match the true needs of the college is a debatable point.

What Do We Bring to the Party? This strategy has become less popular with the decline of some major computer corporations. However, in its prime, colleges sought partnerships with vendors. In order to entice the vendors, colleges promised to accomplish certain goals. The vendors required that the colleges earn their allocation of equipment and software by working on some special projects that they favored. It was difficult for community colleges to get the attention of the vendors compared with some four-year colleges and universities, and it was difficult for community colleges to bring attractive resources to the partnership.

Everybody Needs to Be Converted. This is a faculty-centered strategy. A college invests in a computer for all faculty members' offices, provides training opportunities, and creates a resource center to support the technology. The focus is on exposing all the faculty to technology in the hopes that they will discover its advantages and proper role. The goal is to move more faculty along the technology adoption curve.

Focus on the Geographically Challenged Student. This strategy involves distance learning technologies. It is based on the delivery of education to people living in remote areas. With the advent of the Internet, computing technology is now a key deliverer of distance learning. The needs of the remote student drive the projects. Because of the state politics of sympathy to remote residents, these projects have a greater chance of funding even though they may serve very few students.

The Computer Is the Object. This strategy focuses on the computer as the object of instruction. Historically, community colleges have provided occupational training on the computer. With the explosion in the number of PCs, community colleges added to the curriculum courses teaching the computer as a tool. Faculty in these curricula were the original adopters of technology and used their expertise to advocate investment strategies that best served their needs.

Go for the Gold. Awards and recognition drive this strategy. Associations, government agencies, and corporations often sponsor awards for outstanding software development. The allure of winning significant recognition on a national level drives colleges to compete with projects that are tailored to the rules of the game and not necessarily to the goals of the institution.

Serve the Noble Cause. This strategy favors projects that have a strong humanitarian appeal. Serving the underserved is a commonly proclaimed mission. The gap between the haves and have-nots is a focus of these strategies. Community colleges believe this strategy fits into their mission of building the community.

Don't Worry, I Am in Charge. Executive leadership often employs this strategy. Leaders are eager to demonstrate their leadership skills and thus they declare certain technology directions. This demonstration of leadership may embody many of the previously described strategies, but it issues from an executive.

Invest in the Narrow and Deep or the Shallow and Wide. The narrow and deep strategy is where technology investment is made quite extensively in only a few curriculum areas. Focusing on the computer as the object is an example of this strategy. The shallow and wide strategy involves giving some technology to large numbers of students. Providing e-mail and Internet access would be examples of this strategy.

Looking for the Biggest Bang for the Buck

These technology investment strategies exist in some form or another at most community colleges. This chapter aims not to discredit them but to use them as a backdrop for introducing another strategy. This new strategy for community colleges centers on a very simple proposition. An old-time computer adage says it all: Invest scarce computer dollars where you get the biggest bang for the buck. Colleges can discover the biggest bang by following student enrollment patterns. Community colleges have evolved into a very stable pattern of enrollment because of student choices or requirements. Paying attention to those choices is being learner-centered.

Twigg (1995) names this new technology investment strategy as the "1 percent solution." She makes the following proposition: "Suppose we decide to increase the learning productivity of not two thousand courses but of a mere twenty-five—about 1 percent of the total. And suppose we set as our goal upgrading the quality of these courses to eliminate attrition and to strengthen substantially the foundation that successful students build on in future courses. Then we can examine how information technology can be employed to accomplish this goal and what kind of support is required to do so" (pp. 16–17).

Charles R. Thomas, one of the founders of the National Center for Higher Education Management Systems (NCHEMS) and author of the center's first data dictionary, describes one of the earlier attempts to study enrollment patterns in 1970–71 with the Induced Course Load Matrix software. This software looked at what courses the students really took in comparison to all those offered in the curriculum. From this information, the Resource Requirements Prediction Model (RRPM) could be built and enrollments could be better predicted. One anticipated outcome was to determine which curricula should receive the larger share of the college resources. This software enjoyed a brief show of interest and then disappeared from the landscape (C. R. Thomas, e-mail message to the author, July 9, 1997).

A Proliferation of Courses. In the meantime, several forces led to a tremendous expansion of curriculum offerings for different reasons. First and foremost was the academic ratchet. That is, faculty drove the expansion of the curriculum by proliferating advanced courses based on their personal preferences (Zemsky, 1994). Second, community college course banks expanded as the colleges sought to meet community needs. Degrees and certificates were added in occupational areas. Remedial programs expanded. Transfer courses changed often to meet matriculation requirements of four-year colleges. Third, as the tuition escalated rapidly at four-year colleges, students increasingly registered for their general education requirement courses at the lower-cost community colleges. Fourth, a greater proportion of the students planned to seek a baccalaureate degree than ever before. Fifth, demographics changed for community colleges—the students are older, more diverse, employed, financially strapped, underprepared, part-time, and have additional life responsibilities beyond getting a college education.

A Concentration of Enrollments. The proliferation of courses led to a startling revelation in the 1990s. At the large, comprehensive community colleges, student enrollments were concentrated in very few courses. In an informal gathering of data from the members of the League for Innovation in Community Colleges it was noted that approximately 50 percent of all enrollments were in twenty-five courses (Waechter, 1996).

At Miami-Dade Community College, the institutional research study (1995a) showed that 44 percent of all enrollments in each semester were in twenty-five courses. Those twenty-five courses were among over two thousand offered. The course bank contained an additional twenty-five hundred courses that were not offered. The analysis at Miami-Dade Community College (1995b) showed that 51 percent of all enrollments were in the top twenty-five courses (2.5 percent of those offered) and 34 percent were in the top ten enrolled courses. Dallas Community College District also showed a 50 percent enrollment pattern in the top twenty-five courses. Those courses in the top twenty-five are not surprising: they are the introductory courses in English, mathematics, psychology, accounting, biology, fitness, speech, and so on. The implications of this enrollment concentration for community colleges are profound because they clearly identify the target audience and courses for technology investment strategies.

An interesting exercise for community college leaders is to take the direct instructional costs of the twenty-five courses, compound costs for inflation, and extend to a ten-year planning horizon. The amount of money to be spent on these courses taught in a nontechnological, traditional format grows alarmingly large. So what better place to look for replacing and saving some costs with technology investments? This is clearly the "biggest bang for the buck." For example, at the Maricopa Community Colleges, the estimated direct instructional costs (which do not include the cost of facilities, overhead, or student support services) for the top twenty-five courses are $45 million currently and will accumulate to $600 million for the next decade. That large an expenditure makes funding for technology an economically wise strategy.

The Crisis in Higher Education. Having identified the top twenty-five courses as the target for technology investment, certain questions need to be answered and principles formulated to take appropriate action. The primary question is, what kind of investments should be made in those courses? Sir John Daniel (1997) in his speech to the American Association of Higher Education (AAHE) national conference described the three components of today's crisis in higher education: not enough access, accelerating cost, and reduced flexibility. These three components provide the focus for investment in the top twenty-five.

Access. Access is a byword of the community college movement. However, community colleges are ensconced in brick-and-mortar facilities located at far enough distances that students experience commuting problems. The most conveniently overlooked cost to community college students is their cost of commuting. Owning a car is almost a prerequisite for admission because public transportation to most community colleges is very limited. Added to this problem is the new reality of students with other life commitments, such as work schedules and family demands. Consequently, access is not as good as advertised in community colleges.

An important strategy is to use technology to make the twenty-five courses more accessible. Delivering the entire course or portions of it to the home, workplace, or a convenient center is strategic. Whereas the original distance learning programs focused on students in remote areas, the new strategies must now include alternative delivery mode for inner-city students. Access to student services must also not be overlooked. Most services to students are on an 8 A.M. to 5 P.M., Monday through Friday schedule. The primary reason behind this schedule is the preference of the employees. Yet, nearly 50 percent of student enrollments are in evening and weekend classes. Full-time faculty work hard politically to preserve their assignments in day classes. Most evening courses are then given to part-time faculty. So here again is another disconnect between employee preference and student need for access to educational services.

Cost. The second component of the crisis is cost. Higher education resembles the health care industry, in which cost increases for services far exceeded inflation. When will the system reach the critical breaking point, as many argue has already happened in health care? Technology has the potential to reduce the costs of at least the top twenty-five courses. In many industries during the last decade, technology has not only reduced costs but improved quality. Higher education has not seriously attempted to lower costs. (The exceptions are the Open University in the United Kingdom, the University of Phoenix, and other large nontraditional colleges.) Introducing technology to courses delivered in a business-as-usual way only adds to the cost, yet that is what has happened with the majority of technology investments. Although the word *reengineering* is in some disfavor with academicians, it is appropriate to apply it when using technology for the top twenty-five courses.

Lack of Flexibility. The third component of the crisis is lack of flexibility. Flexibility is a time-honored tradition in community colleges in order to maintain standards. Yet, lack of flexibility stops the curriculum from being current and the schedule of classes from being cost-effective and learner-centered. With the emphasis now on lifelong learning, flexibility is required for adding value to the students. Technology, no doubt, can play a major role in providing the flexibility in terms of when, where, and how students engage in learning.

The Response of Maricopa Community Colleges

At the Maricopa Community Colleges, many technology investments are focusing on Twigg's "1 percent solution" to address this crisis. One of its colleges, Rio Salado College, has developed thirty-five courses on the Internet. Rio Salado used the top twenty-five courses as the guide to select courses for this kind of development. The courses are now available to students around the world and have become a fundamental part of the future of Rio Salado College. The investment (including for faculty salaries, support mechanisms, and equipment) in the top twenty-five courses is seen as learner-centered rather than faculty- or bureaucracy-centered. The college seeks to have an impact on as many students as possible and to improve their learning in the areas they really wish to pursue. It is listening to the customer's choice. It is meeting the real needs of an enlarged community.

Sixty-four percent of the students enrolled in the top twenty-five courses at Maricopa satisfactorily complete the courses with a grade of C or better. What other organization is permitted to discard more than one-third of its possible customers? In community colleges, many of those same noncompleting students take the course again. Needless to say, the cost implications are significant in terms of more sections, more classroom space, and more faculty needed to handle those who reenroll.

To address the retention problem in the top twenty-five courses, Maricopa has invested a large amount of funds and staff time in the reengineering of some of the student support processes, changing policies, and developing new software for what is called the learner-centered system (LCS). Two key innovations to come out of the LCS effort were (1) the design of a learning plan for students to enable them to navigate through their curriculum to attain their educational goals with greater access to the information they need to succeed, and (2) the creation of more flexible scheduling in services that enables these students of the information age to break away from the scheduling of the agricultural age.

The outcome is encouraging. The biggest-bang-for-the-buck approach has helped Maricopa Community Colleges to enhance their learner-centered academic program and to support their students better. This technological investment strategy is a winning one for both these institutions and their students.

References

Daniel, J. S. "Why Universities Need Technology Strategies." *Change,* July–Aug. 1997, pp. 10–17.

Massy, W. F., and Zemsky, R. "Using Information Technology to Enhance Academic Productivity." *EDUCOM Review,* Jan.–Feb. 1996, pp. 12–14.

Miami-Dade Community College. *Districtwide FTSE Report,* 1995a.

Miami-Dade Community College. *CCPF Research File, College-Level Courses Generating the Highest Total Credits Closing Fall Term,* 1995b.

Mobley, L., and McKeown, K. *Beyond IBM.* New York: McGraw-Hill, 1989.

Twigg, C. "One Percent Solution." *EDUCOM Review,* Nov./Dec. 1995, pp. 16–17.

Waechter, W. F. Oral report to the League for Innovation in Community Colleges, Phoenix, Ariz. Dec. 1996.

Zemsky, R. (sr. ed.) "To Dance with Change." *Policy Perspectives,* Apr. 1994, p. 10A.

RONALD D. BLEED *is vice chancellor, information technologies, Maricopa Community Colleges.*

What can be accomplished when faculty take responsibility for using technology appropriately and creatively in the classroom? Initiatives under way at Kirkwood Community College suggest positive outcomes and future possibilities.

Humanizing the Integration of Technology

Terry J. Moran, Michele Payne

Technology can improve learning by improving communication and individualization and by enabling us, as teachers and learners, to hear more voices and reach new listeners. Through technology, we can have access to more multicultural, multidisciplinary information and artifacts than ever before possible: music, film, art, and literature are all available on small circles of plastic we can carry in our pockets. Technology offers us appealing new publication and communication forums: with the World Wide Web, for example, we can speak in relative privacy to an individual on the other side of the world or experience the immediate gratification of sharing what we know with a potential readership of millions through our Web sites. How can we resist taking advantage of these opportunities for ourselves and our students?

Yet many of us on community college campuses remain indifferent to the technology that would help us become better teachers and learners. Our pedagogical culture is text-based and linear, whereas the technology culture is icon-based and intuitive. We experience this culture gap whenever we pick up the documentation for a new piece of software and try to apply what we are reading to what we want to make happen on our computer screen. The linear documentation provided with the software is the type of text academics are often most comfortable dealing with, but it is not useful in teaching us the intuitive, assertive actions we need to be productive with a software program or on the Internet. Linear documentation can define the terms and outline the protocols, but it cannot teach us what we need to know to navigate the technological resources already available or create our own.

Faculty commonly turn to the co-workers who are perceived to have the most information about computers and how they work and to the technicians who support all the computer efforts on campus, from the student record system to the library catalogue. Sensible faculty members don't expect these programmers and technicians to be experts in pedagogical methods or knowledgeable about the subject matter the faculty members teach. Their simple hope is that if they come up with a good idea, the programmer can implement it and the technician can support it. The process is linear and differentiated: first the faculty member supplies the imagination, then the programmer and the technician supply the labor.

Here at Kirkwood, a college of just over ten thousand students located in eastern Iowa, that approach was business as usual for several years, until faculty, programmers, and technicians alike recognized several fundamental flaws:

- There can never be enough programmers and technicians to go around, no matter how many are hired.
- Faculty speak a different language than programmers and technicians do (in the same way that software documentation speaks a different language than the software itself does).
- When the tasks of faculty and programmer are too differentiated, the finished product is often not what the faculty member had in mind. The medium tends to take over the message when it comes to electronic courseware.

Faculty Involvement

Recognizing the important role of technology in bettering the working lives of faculty and improving the educational outcomes for students has always been a part of the Kirkwood culture. It was one of the colleges in the country to introduce a live, interactive instructional television network early on. Kirkwood's president, other administrators, and faculty have twice campaigned successfully in the seven-county district the college serves for technology levies, which now total 9 percent. Aggressive partnering with local industries has resulted in more technology on campus with less capital outlay. The faculty shift toward integrating technology into their everyday lives, assuming both ownership of the technology and responsibility for using it appropriately and imaginatively to enrich their classrooms, is part and parcel of our institutional culture today. We consider faculty ownership and involvement as the way to humanize the integration of technology.

Evidence can be found in four initiatives implemented at the college in the past two years: Instructional Computing Services, offering software and Internet courses to faculty in a high-end computer classroom dedicated to that use; the Instructional Technology Teaching/Learning Improvement Initiative; the Instructional Technology Advisory Committee; and a faculty mentoring program in the use of computer-based diagnostic testing and developmental software.

Instructional Computing Services.   One of Kirkwood's earliest initiatives was creating the Instructional Computing Services department and staffing it with "translators"—four trainers, not technicians, who could serve as liaisons between faculty and the technology. Requirements for the trainers included degrees in instructional design or other educational fields and experience in teaching computer software to adults in the workplace. Working from the philosophy that knowledge is power, and knowing that by fall 1997 every faculty member would have a computer on his or her desk, the Instructional Computing staff began designing courses for the software that faculty were most interested in using: Word, PowerPoint, MS Mail, and Excel. When a new server allowed each office a connection to the Internet, courses in surfing the Web and using it as a classroom resource were added. As faculty became more skilled in the basics, courses in dressing up PowerPoint presentations with audio and video were offered, as were courses in copyright issues as they relate to electronic media, and courses in other, more sophisticated, applications of the Microsoft Office software. A specific sequence of courses in PowerPoint, file management, copyright, and electronic communication was created for and required of instructors designing courses for distance delivery via the Internet. Each course taught is supplemented by handouts designed by the trainers specifically to meet the immediate needs of the Kirkwood faculty. For example, the Excel course in designing a gradebook focuses just on that, not on other uses for Excel such as creating graphs; there is a separate course for that.

The courses are held in a classroom with only ten student stations where the computers and peripherals, with one exception, are kept state of the art. The exception is an older model computer, which is used by faculty to test the functionality of the course work they design and thus ensure its accessibility to more students. Faculty also use the classroom as a workroom for large projects or for projects requiring peripherals not available in their offices. Included among the projects are a PowerPoint presentation on conflict management using video and audio clips, a Web page tutorial on the sources of state and local laws, and a Web page of essays and photographs about their homelands created by international students as part of their ESL course work. Faculty have also developed and offered new courses that involve the students with technology every class period, including an introduction to multimedia course and a second semester multimedia composition course. Altogether, in 1996–97, 214 sections of thirty-eight unique courses were conducted by Instructional Computing Services, with 348 enrollments from a full-time faculty of two hundred.

Instructional Technology Teaching/Learning Initiative. The goal of the Instructional Technology Teaching/Learning Initiative is improving student learning. Now in its second year, the initiative's success in drawing more faculty to technology is a result of placing leadership for integration in the hands of the faculty rather than with administrators or technicians. Two faculty members were selected from several applicants to the Instructional Technology Advisory Committee (see next section). Each received three hours of release time per week in a semester to initiate and support the use of technology in classrooms. The projects generated by this initiative have included a daylong technology fair, six individual faculty projects, and summer institutes for faculty interested in developing Web pages or multimedia to enhance their courses.

The Technology Fair. This fair showcased the work of Kirkwood faculty who have incorporated electronic elements into their courses and included demonstrations of software packages such as Authorware, sessions offering tips for researching topics on the Internet, and testimonials from teachers in the process of adapting their courses for Internet delivery. One outcome of the fair has been that faculty now turn to other faculty for ideas and assistance. A second fair will be held next spring, and among the presenters will be those faculty who submitted proposals and received compensation for developing classroom projects, such as the Web page where international students share their biographies and information about their homelands; the Center for On-Line Writing Assistance (the Kirkwood COW); an interactive tutorial posted to the Kirkwood home page that provides supplementary information on the sources of American law; and a PowerPoint presentation that uses audio and video clips to illustrate conflict management techniques.

Summer Institutes. The weeklong summer institutes will provide training and hands-on experience to ten faculty members who wish to design Web pages or multimedia presentations using PowerPoint to enhance their classroom presentations. Instruction will be presented by Kirkwood's Instructional Computing training coordinator in the mornings, and in the afternoon the coordinator and experienced faculty will be available to assist as the faculty develop their projects.

Instructional Technology Advisory Committee. Although originally convened to "assist in efforts to develop faculty understanding of potential computer applications for education," the Instructional Technology Advisory Committee focused most of its early efforts on prioritizing the acquisition and placement of computer hardware. Now, although questions about hardware purchases are still brought to this faculty committee whose sixteen members represent all instructional areas of the college, its activities are more appropriately focused on identifying ways technology can enrich course content, increase faculty productivity, and improve student outcomes. Recent activities originated by committee members include an institute funded by the National Endowment for the Humanities this summer to study the impact of technology on literature and the development of a software program to allow instructors to download grades from Excel directly into the student record system.

Faculty Mentoring. As part of Kirkwood's Title III grant activity, "Increasing Student Success," faculty from the developmental education department work with faculty in other departments to design curricula for basic skills preparation using software available through Project SYNERGY Integrator (PSI), which is described in Chapter Seven of this volume. The result of this collaboration among departments will be a sequence of courses designed for specific vocational and college preparatory areas; Academic Prep for Agricultural Science is one example. Developmental education faculty are also working with faculty in the health sciences department to determine appropriate prior levels of knowledge for admission into specific programs. Using the American College Testing Program's (ACT) computer-based diagnostic test Compass, cutoff scores will be determined and underprepared students will be directed to appropriate remedial PSI software or developmental courses. This systematic intervention should greatly reduce the number of students feeling lost in the courses through inappropriate placement. Once results of the pilot with health sciences have been studied, the project will be extended to other vocational areas.

Looking Toward the Future

Our faculty anticipate many more opportunities for using technology appropriately and imaginatively to improve student learning. For example, beginning fall 1997, we began a three-year project to identify our riskiest distance-delivered courses and to design advising and academic interventions that can be delivered electronically to improve outcomes for our most isolated learners. We continue to find that we make the most significant technological progress when faculty are empowered to use technology themselves, to drive the initiatives, and to take the responsibility for exemplary practices in and out of the classroom.

TERRY J. MORAN is vice president, Instruction, Kirkwood Community College, Cedar Rapids, Iowa.

MICHELE PAYNE is director, Guided Self-Study, Kirkwood Community College, Cedar Rapids, Iowa.

This chapter describes the journey Montgomery County Community College has taken from its initial computer systems to a collegewide network and also discusses the impact of these changes on the college and the community.

Planning Comprehensively and Implementing Incrementally in an Age of Tightening Budgets

John P. Mastroni, Celeste Marie Schwartz

Montgomery County Community College, located in Blue Bell, Pennsylvania, is a comprehensive community college dedicated to serving the entire community. The college offers a wide range of academic programs both for transfer students and for career-minded students, as well as certificate and lifelong learning programs. In addition, the college is dedicated to assisting community business and industry in training and retraining employees. Addressing the needs of its community has helped the college experience considerable growth over the last several years. The keystone of Montgomery County Community College's philosophy is a commitment to student success.

The College and Its Dilemma

Montgomery County Community College, formally founded on December 8, 1964, is the sixth largest of the fourteen community colleges created under the terms of the Pennsylvania Community College Act of 1963. The college offers over fifty transfer and career programs leading to associate degrees and certificates. Over nine thousand students are currently enrolled in its daytime and evening classes, which are served by 170 full-time and 300 part-time faculty, 70 administrators, and 230 support staff. The Central Campus is in Blue Bell, Pennsylvania, halfway between Norristown and Lansdale and some twenty-five miles northwest of center-city Philadelphia. A second full-service campus, the West Campus, located in the borough of Pottstown, opened in fall 1996.

Early Automation Efforts. Beginning in the late 1970s, the college's administrative functions were automated with IBM mainframe equipment. The 256 terminals throughout the campus were supported by coaxial cables, as opposed to fiber optics. In the late 1980s, the college's chief information officer initiated an ambitious telecommunications plan that detailed the cable and equipment foundations needed to advance the institution toward conventional networking. Throughout the early 1990s, this plan began to come to fruition, although not in the most logical order. The plan had been conceived of and was even modified during these years as a comprehensive whole, but it could not be put into place that way. Acquiring funding for some pieces proved easier than for others. Therefore, it was decided to implement each part as funding became available. Segments of the plan were funded through the college budget and grants. As a result, what emerged did not always seem like a plan coming together but rather like a less-than-coherent series of purchases, installations, and services.

Local Area Networks. By 1992, the college had acquired seven local area network (LAN) student laboratories on campus. These labs were centered around the IBM Classroom LAN Administration System (ICLAS) and Local Area Network Kit (LANkit) utilities and offered "shrink-wrapped" network lab services to several academic departments on campus. Although these packaged networks were popular among academic institutions at the time, they proved to have several drawbacks. Each lab was being used by a single department and had its own file server with a base of installed applications. Generic IDs were used to grant students access to the systems. The systems provided inefficient use of equipment, support resources, and faculty and student time. Attempting to replicate services, such as office applications—for example, word processing, databases, and spreadsheets—computer programming applications, and tutorials on stand-alone equipment and a series of LANs was wasteful and inefficient. The college quickly realized that its initial, fragmented approach to providing computer service was no longer practical.

The Plan and Its Promises

With the many possibilities for cost savings that an integrated system offered, the college launched a new project with a primary goal of allowing access to all network resources from any workstation on campus via one ID. The plan called for an integrated technical infrastructure. Its components were creating a collegewide network; connecting all computers to the network; allowing access from anywhere in the network to any service on the network; providing security and privacy; and accomplishing the goals at a reasonable cost.

The access issue involved ensuring that all students would have available to them any software they would need for any course they would take. The college also wanted to make e-mail and the Internet available to all students and staff. This would have been virtually impossible with a series of unconnected LANs. With access came other issues, such as security and support. A system needed to be devised that would prevent corruption by any user.

Anticipated Savings on Equipment. The cost of maintaining as many as sixteen LANs (the estimated number necessary at present to serve all student labs and administrative offices) serviceable only on-site would have been prohibitive. Replicating the majority of the academic software on even a substantial percentage of these computers in LANs would have been beyond the purchasing capacity of the college. And the cost of separate servers for sixteen labs would have been approximately $96,000, whereas the cost of the two servers needed for the wide area network (WAN) is only $40,000.

Anticipated Savings on Technical Support. Also, the technical support personnel under the old system of expansion would have required an increase of at least 150 percent, from the equivalent of four full-time positions to the equivalent of ten. Reduced staffing under the integrated system is possible because software is located in one area, adjacent to the staff offices, which the staff can get to easily instead of having to go to each LAN site to deal with problems that require such attention. With the WAN, in which every computer is connected to the same network, many problems can be corrected from the staff person's desk.

The staffing component would bring with it other, less direct savings. For instance, various members of the staff have been certified by several of the vendors who supply the college's hardware and software. This allows the staff to work on many problems that would otherwise have to be handled by company representatives at a per-visit or per-hour cost. In some instances, it even reduces the cost of service contracts. For example, two staff members have been certified by Compaq, which has resulted in a savings of $15,000 on the contract for the Compaq servers used by the college.

The Implementation and Its Realities

As the title of this chapter suggests, although the planning was comprehensive, the implementation was incremental and contingent on the availability of resources. Phase I focused on the infrastructure and Phase II on software.

Phase I. A National Science Foundation (NSF) grant, awarded in 1992, supplied the college with Internet connectivity via a leased 19.2 Kbps circuit through JvNCNet. Installation of the circuit was completed in mid-1993. The college acquired a Cisco AGS+ token-ring router that has been used as the backbone of all college networking and has allowed for the connection of several student networks on campus as well as a dedicated Internet circuit. Also in 1993, the college contracted with Bell Atlantic Network Integration to install a collegewide fiber infrastructure as well as core networking hardware (token-ring router and hub equipment). This infrastructure enabled connectivity among all existing independent LANs.

IBM's Professional Office System software (PROFS) was still being used as the primary campus e-mail system because not all users had been converted to networked PCs. Many of the PC users, however, asked for Internet e-mail access. Pegasus mail, with its SMTP gateway as a means of temporarily supplying this service, was used. In the same year, a search started for a system that would replace the many "homegrown" CICS COBOL applications the college administration used at that time. By mid-1994, bandwidth limitations were realized and the circuit was upgraded to 56 Kbps.

In fall 1994, a token-ring switch was purchased to alleviate student lab bandwidth strains. Each lab was supplied with its own 16 Mbps segment, and file server connections were made using a Fiber Distributed Data Interface (FDDI) module on the switch. The first Netware file server strictly for staff use was also installed in late 1994. Shared applications, such as Microsoft Office, were installed and provided to college administrators and staff. Print servers were installed to provide work group access to laser printers. Software metering was used to limit the number of legal copies of all applications. A Netware for Systems Applications Architecture (SAA) terminal gateway was used to provide connectivity to the existing mainframe while limiting network and client protocol support to Internet Package eXchange (IPX) and IP.

The initial stage of the project was completed in fall 1994. All networked labs were collapsed into the Standard Microsystems Corporation (SMC) switch and serviced via only one Netware file server. Over eighty DOS and Windows version 3.1 applications were installed on a large Compaq file server. These included core applications, such as Microsoft Office, e-mail, and Internet utilities as well as the "vertical," course-specific applications. Menu support, file distribution, and Windows INI management were done via the Saber LAN workstation product. An automated system was developed to assist in the process of creating over thirty-five hundred student IDs based on registration information in the database. Students and faculty were given shared and private storage space to promote the use of file sharing and distribution. An e-mail system was installed to allow for student-to-faculty-to-Internet messaging for the first time in the college's history.

As the system began to be used, the success of the changes implemented became evident. Many students and faculty praised the benefits that the system offered. Some faculty started to collect homework via e-mail. Labs began to be cross-scheduled between the many departments utilizing computer services. Faculty members accessed all student applications using their office computers.

Phase II. In 1995, the Datatel Colleague software package was chosen. Information technology (IT) staff as well as user representatives from all departments evaluated the software. A conversion that the vendor scheduled to take twenty-four months from the old, homegrown database system to Datatel was accomplished in an unprecedented six months. The college was chosen as a test site for the next release of the software. It is expected that this release will be applied this summer. The network played an important role in these conversions, allowing simultaneous and smooth transition from mainframe access via the SAA gateway to UNIX host access via the IP stack on all administrative clients.

In summer 1995, a CD-ROM server with a six-station network was installed in the learning resources center. The equipment was installed as part of an effort to improve our students' access to information resources on campus as well as to a growing number of documents available only on CDs. The CD-ROM network provides more effective access to electronic indexes, full-text newspapers, and government documents. Internet access is also available on these machines. The access to these resources is available not only to the college community but to county residents as well.

This design is resourceful, providing increased security, bandwidth, and connectivity where needed while reutilizing existing equipment elsewhere on the network. And the college has been providing traditional services, such as file, print, messaging, and Internet, to the student population since the completion of the project. Netware file servers have been the mainstay throughout the life of the college network.

As part of a U.S. Department of Education Title III grant, in fall 1995 the college created a multimedia-based computer lab for self-paced courses in writing, math, and reading. Although this lab functions primarily from a dedicated server containing discipline-specific software for instruction, it is also attached to the college's network, enabling students registered in these self-paced courses to access all other relevant college network services.

The Title III project has also funded a library automation system that provides the student or county residents with a graphical user interface (GUI) from which catalog searches and other library research can be done. The system is accessible at our new campus and will provide services there as well.

In conjunction with the Title III project, the college became a regional training center for Project SYNERGY, a national developmental education project based at Miami-Dade Community College (described in Chapter Seven of this volume). This software is used primarily in the Title III lab. Central to Montgomery County Community College's participation in this project is its ability to make all Project SYNERGY software available to its faculty and students from any computer station, that is, classrooms, the learning assistance lab, the developmental studies lab, and faculty offices.

In late 1995, the institution felt the strains from both the academic and administrative sides in regard to outdated workstations. To solve this problem, using money from the college's fund balance, the president decided to upgrade the twelve student labs on campus to Pentium 90 PCs. The academic networking equipment was upgraded as well. A conversion from token-ring to ethernet was made. The new configuration includes 10/100 PCI NIC cards, work group switches for each lab that supplies a dedicated 10 Mbps segment to each lab workstation, as well as a fast ethernet uplink to a backbone switch. The token-ring equipment and PCs are being reused in administrative and faculty offices throughout the campus.

In the 1996 spring semester, the college offered its first set of on-line courses via a bulletin board system (BBS), including courses in accounting and economics. Feedback was positive, and since then courses in accounting, economics, English, history, and psychology have been offered. (In fall 1997, additional courses in philosophy and the Internet were scheduled.) The system can be accessed by modem, college WAN, or the Internet.

The increased use of e-mail by faculty, students, and staff soon showed the limitations of the Pegasus package, especially with the need for additional features, such as calendaring and scheduling. Therefore, in June 1996 the Novell GroupWise product, which offers DOS and Windows support for messaging, calendaring, scheduling, and forms processing, has been used.

The college phone system (an AT&T Dimension 400) had been outdated for many years. In 1996, the college installed a new telecommunications system that serves both campuses and includes Private Branch eXchange (PBX) equipment, voicemail, fax server, remote access server, personal videoconferencing equipment, and classroom videoconferencing systems. Installation of these systems has begun.

When the West Campus was built in 1996, WAN services were needed across campuses for the first time at the college. We are purchasing a new router to support the communications links. A Cisco model 7505 router will be used to connect the administrative and academic networks on the Central Campus to the West campus and the Internet. It will become the backbone of two separately switched networks and will shield the administrative services from student lab, Internet, and dial-up users.

The college has been in the process of acquiring new PBX equipment for both its Central and West campuses. During this acquisition period, a new structured copper plant will be installed at both campuses. Every workstation will be equipped with a CAT 5 outlet for data use. Voice communications will be made over an additional CAT 3 termination in the modular outlet.

Internet access and TCP/IP stacks are available on most PCs used by students. For example, FTP, TELNET, GOPHER, and WWW are supported. All faculty and college staff with computers have TCP/IP support on their computers because the protocol is necessary for access to a new administrative software system, which operates on a UNIX platform. Training sessions on e-mail use and Internet browsing offered through the college's professional development center have proved very successful. The Internet has become a valuable resource for college staff, faculty, and students.

In addition to the progress described here, one other element not anticipated at the inception of the conversion project was meeting the needs of students with disabilities in compliance with the Americans with Disabilities Act (ADA). As the number of students with disabilities attending the college grew, so did the need for various means of assisting them with technology. To date, necessary accommodations have not had a direct impact on the structure of the campus network but only in helping students access the network services. The college now provides workstations that meet ADA height and accessibility requirements and contain various adaptive hardware and software. Voice synthesizers, text-to-speech converters, adaptive keyboards, and large monitors have been purchased. Screen magnifying and reduced keystroke software have also been installed on many of these computers. Funding for these purchases has generally come from Carl Perkins grant funds.

The Results and Their Implications

It must be noted that although the results of the college's move to the wide area network are generally positive there have also been some negatives.

Positives. In the period from 1980 to 1990, before the change to the WAN, the college had a maximum of 250 computers. Software was limited academically to some DOS-based computer languages and science and mathematics applications. Administratively, it was limited to IBM's PROFS system and a DOS-based accounting package. Today on the two campuses there are approximately 830 computers and over 200 academic Windows-based software packages in such additional areas as anatomy and physiology, art, astronomy, biology, chemistry, education, English, foreign languages, marketing, nursing, political science, reading, and speech. Administratively, Novell's GroupWise and Datatel's Colleague packages are used. Shared software and metering has allowed us to keep those costs in line. For example, at $54 a copy, placing the Microsoft Office product in all academic student labs as well as on faculty, administrator, and support staff desktops would have cost approximately $43,000. However, because everyone does not actually need access to these products simultaneously, it was possible with the WAN configuration to license only 275 copies at a cost of $14,850. And the staff increased only a little over 35 percent to one part-time and six full-time people in the integrated approach, for a savings of approximately $122,500 a year in salaries plus benefit costs.

Other savings brought about by the network are the reduction in the number of high-quality printers installed and, therefore, the ability to provide more powerful computers to faculty and staff than would otherwise have been possible. People without a laser printer, that is, those with a dot matrix or ink jet printer directly attached to their computers, can send appropriate print jobs to one of sixty shared laser printers. Another benefit derives from the savings in technical support. Obviously, the ability to install software on one server is more efficient than installing on multiple servers located in several buildings. Also, with the WAN, the staff of the computer center can often solve problems from their desks or, at worst, at the server located just down the hall, rather than having to go to the LAN site. This is also a direct benefit to students and faculty, because problems can usually be solved more quickly than was previously the case.

In preparing this chapter, the authors interviewed nine faculty members now using the college's computer facilities, four members of the college's Web team, and staff members of the computer center. The primary purpose of those interviews was to discover the level of satisfaction with the facilities' capabilities from the perspectives of both users and support staff.

Faculty and students access the network in several ways: first, in one of the twelve classroom computer labs for primary course work; second, in the learning assistance lab for supplemental work (CAI and programs); third, in the Title III-funded developmental studies lab for alternative delivery of pre-college-level courses in English, math, and reading; and fourth, remotely, via the Internet and the college's BBS. Also, over the last three years, the college has created a number of portable multimedia carts equipped with computer, CD-ROM drive, VHS videocassette player, sound system, and projection system, which can be used in any classroom since all classrooms have been connected to the WAN via an ethernet jack. In addition, faculty have access to the multimedia development lab, also funded by Title III, in which they can create their own multimedia presentations and lessons for use in their classes or in the learning assistance lab.

Benefits noted by instructors include consistency in the look and operation of equipment and software, which was made possible only by the move to the WAN. Previously, software availability, menu designs, and hardware specifications depended on the room in which the instructor was working. Now, all labs and carts have all of the college software available, and menu design and hardware are standardized. Because all student computers as well as the multimedia carts connect directly to the network server, students and faculty can access any program from anywhere, and all carts are equipped with the same hardware: Pentium computer, CD-ROM drive, VHS videocassette player, sound system, and projection device.

A nursing instructor has found that the multimedia presentations convey the same information better, allowing her to present what used to be a six-hour lecture in much less time—approximately four hours. She has also found that students "get it better," a conclusion validated by test results and clinical application.

Another implication of this major technological change was the increased importance of training for faculty and staff. Members of the IT staff offer workshops to faculty, administrators, and support staff on various aspects of the system. These workshops are coordinated by the college's professional development center. The center also works individually with interested faculty and staff to help them develop special projects. This training is part of the normal duties of the IT staff and, therefore, does not entail an additional expense.

Negatives. The problems generally fall into two categories: those that do not fit the overall plan and those that emerge from the benefits of the plan. In the first category, some software used in courses is not designed to be networked. Although IT staff have attempted to find ways to make this software function from the network, their efforts have been only partially successful. At least part of each of these software packages must be locally installed. The effect has been to limit access to specific machines, thus hindering the overall plan of universal access. This has caused problems in course scheduling because the college has been attempting to move away from the use of discipline-specific labs. For example, computer graphics courses can be offered only in specific labs in which the necessary software is installed, limiting the use of those labs. Retrofitting is not an easy task.

The second set of problems, perhaps easier to deal with, arises from the positive reaction to the new system. Faculty members interviewed for this chapter who are currently using the technology have noted, for example, that the multimedia carts they use for their classroom presentations are becoming so popular that they cannot always get one when they need one. And the success of the plan to date has led to more faculty members using technology as an integral part of their curriculum. This has increased dramatically the number of students needing access to computers and, therefore, has created logjams when students try to access computers to do their assignments, despite an increase of over 30 percent in the number of student computers in the last three years. Even more importantly, the number of computer labs has not only increased from nine to twelve but the computers in the older labs have now been upgraded, with Pentium 90s serving as the new standard.

The most basic problem the college must address concerns adequate access for students, faculty, and staff. The initial step to solve this problem was taken at the start of the fall 1997 semester. As originally configured, the WAN accommodated only 250 users at the same time. The installation of an upgraded server and the move to Novell 4.11 has increased the capacity to approximately 500 academic and administrative users.

The Future and Its Demands

The future of computing on campus must be examined from two perspectives: short-term and long-term.

Short-Term Plans. Short-term plans concern immediate needs arising from continual upgrades to applications and the increased use of technology by faculty and students. As faculty continue to integrate technology into their courses, future demands on the resources will include additional permanent multimedia presentation stations; the creation of student newsgroups accessed through the college's Web page; the expansion of Internet-based courses (eventually replacing the current BBS courses); the transmission of multimedia programs to remote sites, including students' homes; increased server space for faculty and students; and constant upgrades of system software to accommodate increasingly powerful applications.

Long-Term Plans. The long-term considerations include the need for greater security, not just to protect hardware and software located on the campuses but also to protect the integrity of the entire network, which will more commonly be accessed by remote users in our county service area, the rest of the country, and even the world. Although the Internet allows a type of interaction never before possible, it also increases the risk that applications and systems attached to it will be tampered with.

Long-term plans must also address the ways in which the college provides access and support to its constituents. As computing becomes less a supplement to the educational experience and more a basic part of it, faculty and students will need constant access to resources. The current means of supplying computer equipment to faculty will not be sufficient. Ordering a multimedia setup to be delivered to a classroom on an occasional basis will be inadequate as more faculty need such equipment daily. The college must find a way to place presentation devices in the majority of classrooms, perhaps supplying faculty with portable computers that they can take to their classes as necessary and simply plug into the projection equipment. But this would mean supplying over 150 full-time faculty with their own laptop computers. The next question is, how do we support adjunct faculty? Furthermore, as computers become more commonplace among our students, we can expect that they will carry hardware with them to their classes and to the learning assistance lab. The college will need to provide network access directly to the students' PCs.

Although we understand that we need to resolve all of these and other issues, we are certain that they will be dealt with in a manner similar to that used in the past: we will do what can be done when it can be done. Despite any grand scheme, implementation will undoubtedly occur one piece at a time as funds are secured.

Conclusion

As can be seen, Montgomery County Community College's vision of the importance of technology in education has helped it to anticipate as well as to keep up with needs. The college has striven to develop a comprehensive plan for the acquisition, maintenance, and upgrading of that technology. However, the fiscal realities have forced the institution to implement that vision in a somewhat ad hoc fashion. Undoubtedly, this will be the trend for the foreseeable future. Delay only breeds delay. We cannot afford to wait for an ideal moment to put into practice our vision but must continue to dedicate resources, steadily and surely, to technology that addresses our constantly changing needs.

JOHN P. MASTRONI is director, Learning Assistance Lab, Montgomery County Community College.

CELESTE MARIE SCHWARTZ is chief information officer, Montgomery County Community College.

*This chapter describes a multi-institutional, multiyear
collaborative project designed to address the problems
associated with underprepared college students. The chapter
discusses the technological products and human processes
that have come together to set the stage for considering technology
integration as an instrument for psychological change.*

Project SYNERGY: An Enduring Collaboration for a Common Cause

Kamala Anandam

In 1989, under the auspices of the League for Innovation in the Community
College, with the leadership of Miami-Dade Community College and the collaboration of IBM, a group of faculty and administrators from community colleges across the nation attended a weeklong meeting at the Biltmore Hotel in
Miami. There they discussed the role of technology in addressing the problems
of underprepared college students. Emerging from this meeting, they under-
stood that there was a need to launch a project with a mission, a vision, and a
passion. Mission and passion were evident among the members of the group
who had worked with underprepared college students for many, many years.
It was the vision that needed a great deal of discussion. What became clear was
that the project should take a holistic approach to and a long-term view of
solutions for problems that have been in the making for several years. It also
became clear that the human aspects of the solution should not be separated
from the technological support. Although it was not evident at the beginning
what the holistic approach would entail, the project has since evolved to
encompass faculty development, technology products, and outcomes evaluation.

Project SYNERGY was launched a year after that meeting with the participation of all eighteen League colleges and four other institutions, including
three four-year universities, and it has expanded since then. The project has

The author gratefully acknowledges the funding provided for this project by IBM, the Federal Department of Education through its Title III grant, and the Florida Department of
Education, and the participation of numerous individuals from several colleges and universities, all of which contributed to its success.

been supported by a $2.6 million hardware grant from IBM, a $2.3 million Title III grant from the U.S. Department of Education, and a $500,000 grant from the Florida Department of Education. The IBM and Florida grants have been shared among participating colleges. Although the financial support for Project SYNERGY is substantial, the time, effort, and expertise contributed by more than five hundred faculty from all participating institutions have been far more significant. The former set the stage for various entities to come together and work together for a common cause; the latter seized the opportunity to harness a collective wisdom and exert an effort in face of the challenge. The essence of synergy, as Covey (1989) points out, is to tolerate differences, compensate for weaknesses, and capitalize on strengths; Project SYNERGY has embodied this essence.

Faculty Development

All the activities associated with faculty development were discipline-based and required teamwork across participating institutions. The result was some useful products for faculty.

Software Review. Project SYNERGY's first activity was to review existing software suitable for use in developmental education. As the first step in this process, faculty drew up a comprehensive list of learning objectives, initially for reading, writing, and math, and later for ESL and for study skills and critical thinking. When a project aims to meet the needs of a number of people, we learned, attempting to achieve consensus is a futile effort; instead, we aimed for comprehensiveness so that if one individual looks for a particular objective, he or she can find it on the list. Project SYNERGY's comprehensive lists include 167 objectives in reading, 82 in writing, 266 in math, 219 in ESL, and 115 in study skills and critical thinking. These learning objectives became a cornerstone for several other activities of the project that followed.

The individuals involved in the software review came from institutions all over the country. The only requirement stipulated by the project staff was that they be involved in teaching underprepared college students. These individuals identified the existing software they wished to review and then indicated, from a practitioner's point of view, which Project SYNERGY objectives were implemented satisfactorily by the software. The project staff used that information to compile a database of reviews of useful software. As the software reviews coordinator said, "A significant and integral feature of the software review process has been the highly positive responses of the faculty doing the grassroots work. They believe that reviewing instructional software for Project SYNERGY has constituted a central activity of their professional development for several reasons: they have learned to evaluate software more critically and systematically; they understand better how to use software with their students; and their stature within their institution as developmental educators has been enhanced" (Kotler, 1993, p. 5).

Question Writing. The second activity was to engage the faculty in writing test questions to match the learning objectives. Faculty teams in reading, writing, mathematics, ESL, and study skills and critical thinking wrote questions to correspond to the Project SYNERGY objectives and then reviewed them for quality and validity. The reading faculty, in addition, selected and created reading passages upon which some comprehension questions were based. At the start of this effort in 1992, the project team prepared and distributed an extensive set of guidelines and sample questions that the question writers and reviewers could follow. Five discipline coordinators at Miami-Dade were responsible for keeping track of the faculty authors' choice of learning objectives for which they wished to write questions, sending the completed items out to other question writers for review, and ultimately accepting (or rejecting) the questions for Project SYNERGY. The project staff was responsible for entering the questions into BANQUE, the computerized test bank system. As of July 1997, seven thousand questions had been entered into BANQUE. The following comments from coordinators speak for faculty development through this discipline-based collaborative activity:

> Over the last two years, I have enjoyed communicating with a number of colleagues from around the country and working with them on the writing of test bank questions for reading. I have appreciated the time and effort many people have put into organizing their expertise into questions that they feel adequately address some of the reading skills that are important for students to master. Personally, I have learned a great deal about question writing and about writing in general from my involvement with this project. Writing questions for students involves attention to word choice, clarity of expression, organization, and appearance. The writing, evaluating, and editing of questions and answer choices that this project has required and the contacts I have had with colleagues from around the country have been valuable experiences for me, both professionally and personally. [Don Meaghre, Miami-Dade Community College, 1995, p. 6]

> One of the most enjoyable aspects of working as a coordinator has been my interaction with faculty as close as the North Campus of Miami-Dade Community College to as far away as Bakersfield College in California. It has been exciting to work with faculty who are contributing to making Project SYNERGY a success. We share a common belief that our students will benefit from the integration of teaching and technology that Project SYNERGY provides. [Melinda Prague, Miami-Dade Community College, 1995, p. 7]

> I have been the discipline coordinator for the mathematics portion of the test bank since its onset. Writing guidelines was my first major task. Once those were completed and sent to the writers, the coordinating began. The greatest joy for me has been the opportunity to work with so many different people from such a variety of places and institutions. I have seen, by the process of writing, revising, and reviewing others' questions, a great deal of improvement in the ability

of some of the writers to interpret objectives and write questions. [Norma Agras, Miami-Dade Community College, 1995, p. 7]

Software Implementation Model. My Software Implementation Model (Miami-Dade Community College, 1992) provides a systematic and long-term structure for faculty to use in integrating technology, teaching, and learning. It is a deviation from workshops that last a day or two. This approach includes the cognitive aspects of human behavior. Based on an internal frame of reference for faculty involvement and action, the model consists of five stages: awareness, analysis, accommodation, assimilation, and adoption, as shown in Figure 7.1.

Generally, faculty are expected to move from the awareness to the adoption stage directly and quickly. The need for analysis has been ignored or underestimated. The analysis stage permits faculty to work through the software as a student might to understand what it does, how it does it, and what implications that has for the faculty's role and the student's curriculum. This task is time consuming and often unlike that of selecting a textbook. With a textbook, an instructor might recognize the author and feel comfortable about adopting it; she might thumb through the table of contents and note that the chapters cover the curriculum, or if she doesn't like a particular chapter, she might decide to ask her students to ignore it. Software does not lend itself to this type of cursory examination and quick decision. More importantly, programming is not linear but branching. Unless faculty members go through all the possible ways of branching, they cannot know what their students will be exposed to when they use the software and, therefore, decide what they will have to do to provide what the software does not or cannot provide. This is why it is critical to go beyond technical support and include support that cov-

Figure 7.1. Software Implementation Model

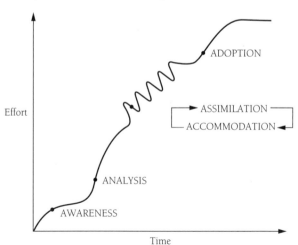

ers the areas of curriculum, teaching, research, and counseling.

The accommodation and assimilation stages are intertwined and together represent the integration process. In simplistic terms, accommodation means that a new piece of information or a new practice is treated in one's mind as peripheral and easily discardable. Assimilation occurs when an individual changes his pattern of mental organization in order to make the new piece of information or practice integral to his way of thinking or behaving. In this instance, it is about teaching, learning, and technology. People cannot expect an overnight miracle when it comes to changing their way of thinking. This process is evolutionary and naturally slow. That is why these two stages, accommodation and assimilation, are represented as a spiral in the Software Implementation Model. In this model, support needs to be provided to faculty one-on-one or in small groups over an extended period of time. Not all faculty follow the model in its entirety. Some quit after the first implementation because the results were not spectacular; some settle for how they used the software the first time even though the outcomes were less than adequate; others keep trying to find ways to improve the outcomes.

Although my Software Implementation Model presents an internal frame of reference for faculty to understand the technology integration process, my Human Encounters with Technology Model (Figure 7.2) provides an external frame of reference for institutions to understand the technology integration process. The stages in this model include the following:

Figure 7.2. Human Encounters with Technology

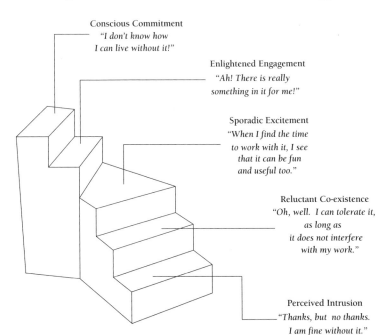

Perceived intrusion of technology as reflected in expressions such as, "Thanks, but no thanks. I am fine without it."

Reluctant coexistence with technology as reflected in expressions such as, "Oh, well! I'll tolerate it as long as it doesn't interfere with my work."

Sporadic excitement about technology as reflected in expressions such as, "Look what it did for me." The excitement is caused, of course, by sporadic involvement.

Enlightened engagement as reflected in expressions such as, "Ah! There is something in it for me."

Conscious commitment as reflected in expressions such as, "I don't know how I can live without it."

An institution's plan for technology integration is likely to benefit from including these two models for the faculty development activities.

Technology Products

The technology products developed under Project SYNERGY were intended to support and facilitate human activities in integrating teaching and technology. The faculty development activities discussed in the previous section indicated the need for the products. The collaborative approach in developing these products contributed significantly to their value. The 149 faculty who reviewed software, 114 faculty who wrote questions, 5 discipline coordinators who managed the question-writing activity, 400 or so faculty members who helped in the functions specifications for the Project SYNERGY Integrator (PSI), and 50 faculty members who evaluated PSI all enhanced the usefulness of these products. With PSI in particular the various perspectives of faculty certainly helped in developing a comprehensive and responsive system.

   Project SYNERGY Integrator. PSI is an open architecture adaptive management system for local area networks (LANs) and wide area networks (WANs). An open architecture allows instructional software from different publishers to operate in the PSI environment as opposed to each software operating as a separate entity requiring separate sign-on by students. The significant contribution of the open architecture is to create an integrated learning environment for the students. The adaptive aspect of PSI allows it to be flexible and responsive to faculty in setting up their courses, and to track students' progress individually and notify faculty about potential problems. On the one hand, PSI provides a system that has standard faculty and student interfaces; on the other, it provides a platform of neutrality to accommodate software from multiple vendors without affecting the standard user interfaces. It incorporates Project SYNERGY learning objectives and mastery test questions. It provides options for faculty to indicate their preferences as to how PSI should manage their courses, to get a more efficient handle on how their students are progressing, and to take appropriate action in a multivendor software environment. Thus, PSI functions like a personal assistant to the instructor. Faculty can use PSI for as many courses as they wish and students can use it for more than one course. Faculty can be teaching different sections of the same course and manage each quite differently if they wish. PSI has a curriculum database—learning objectives database, which currently includes objectives for reading, writing, math, ESL, and study skills and critical thinking; a diagnostic assessment database, which includes American College Testing's (ACT) Compass, a program consisting of tests that help provide students with direction in planning their college careers; a test bank (BANQUE) database, whose items are keyed to the learning objectives; and a software database, which includes PSI-compatible software and resources that the user chooses to install under PSI (the software and resources are linked to the learning objectives). These linkages are important in providing a seamless learning environment for the students. It guides the students through their curriculum plans and provides smooth transitions for them from one learning objective to another and from one software package to another. In other words, PSI functions like a personal tutor.

By design, PSI is capable of functioning like an instrument of change in the teaching and learning environment. Educators will be able to examine PSI's detailed records in relation to the students' progress throughout the semester. They will also be able to orchestrate the use of human and technological resources to help the students better. In addition, they will be able to question the traditional practices for delivering courses to determine which of those can be altered because of PSI's capabilities.

Concerning the software vendors, PSI will enable them to become more attuned to the potential of collaborative efforts such as Project SYNERGY to further their own cause. They will see the benefit of encouraging such projects with their support—both moral and financial—and thus have an inside track toward developing and marketing their products. It is hoped that they will be prompted to evaluate their often costly efforts to maintain and market management and instructional systems, and then to consider focusing on quality instructional modules that operate in a networked environment. Last, they will learn that coexistence with their competitors is necessary if they wish to reach a critical mass in the educational community. For the students, PSI provides an on-line curriculum plan, instruction, and testing, along with an on-line record of their progress and time-on-task. PSI will enable the students to take charge of their own learning and monitor their own progress.

BANQUE. BANQUE is an integral component of PSI. In the PSI environment, when BANQUE is called upon to produce a topic test, it randomly selects items from the database to match the specific objectives covered by the topic for that student. The number of items it selects per objective is governed by what the faculty specify. BANQUE administers the test on-line to each student, scores the test, shows the results, and indicates which items were answered correctly or incorrectly. Students use these as practice tests to prepare for the College-Level Academic Skills Test (CLAST).

Outcomes Evaluation

We recognized early on that technology has a definite role to play in a comprehensive solution that addresses the issue of underprepared college students. Rather than focus on technology alone, the question we chose to address was, What combination of human and technological resources will yield the best results? In Project SYNERGY, faculty used outcomes evaluation as a tool to guide them through their own integration of technology with their own teaching. Meaningful and enduring uses of software emerge when each faculty member applies an internal frame of reference. Giving faculty the time and encouraging them to explore the software from their personal perspectives sets the stage for them to engage in self-evaluation and identify ways to improve how they teach and how they use the software. We found this to be true among our faculty, with some looking inwardly more than others. Bloom's idea (Bloom, Hastings, and Madaus, 1971) of formative evaluation eased the faculty into taking responsibility for self-evaluation and self-improvement. According to Bloom, "Formative evaluation is for us the use of systematic evaluation in the process of curriculum construction, teaching, and learning for the purpose of improving any of these three processes. Since formative evaluation takes place during the formation stage, every effort should be made to use it to improve the process. This means that in formative evaluation, one must strive to develop the kinds of evidence that will be most useful in the process, seek the most useful method of reporting the evidence, and search for ways of reducing the negative effect associated with evaluation—perhaps by reducing the judgmental aspects of evaluation or, at the least, by having the users of the formative evaluation (teachers, students, curriculum makers) make the judgments. The hope is that the users of the formative evaluation will find ways of relating the results of evaluation to the learning and instructional goals they regard as important and worthwhile" (p. 117).

We have encouraged faculty to use formative evaluation as an instrument for change and not as a litmus test of good teaching. Individual case studies and summaries can be found in Project SYNERGY's *Software Implementation* and *Year Two, Year Three,* and *Year Four* reports (Miami-Dade Community College, 1991, 1992, 1993, 1995), available in ERIC.

The outcomes evaluation process is greatly enhanced by PSI because it can be used differently from one class to another while maintaining an accurate record of each student's transactions with the Integrator. The available diagnostic and topic tests, e-mail, software usage reports, student time-on-task reports (time spent in working through their curriculum plan), and computer games as rewards for effort and achievement (passing a topic test) make it possible for faculty to test PSI's impact in various configurations.

The faculty who participated in the studies have expressed their belief in the potential of technology to help their students and their disappointment when the outcomes do not match their expectations. In spite of some disappointments, several continue to explore better ways to incorporate PSI in their courses. Some observations over the last four years in conducting evaluation studies include the following:

"It's the students' enthusiasm and motivation that win the faculty over to stay with the implementation of technology."

"Attempting to improve students' retention and success rates at the same time has occasionally yielded unexpected results. In some studies, it was observed that when retention rates were improved, the reverse was true for success rates as reflected by the end-of-term grades assigned by the faculty. It could be that some students may require longer than a semester to succeed; or that the grade was based on more than what PSI covered."

"Training and support for integrating technology in the learning environment need to be provided on a long-term basis at the departmental level, and they should be discipline-based."

"The individual who provides the training and support needs to possess good interpersonal skills, especially listening skills; to understand curricular requirements and faculty goals; to be knowledgeable about how the hardware/software works; and to be skillful in conducting evaluation studies. In Project SYNERGY, this individual is called a software implementation designer to signify a role quite different from that of an instructional designer."

Conclusion

Project SYNERGY was conceptualized and implemented as a collaborative project. It has been the right project at the right time for the right reasons. It has had the right players who asked the right questions and knew at least some of the right answers. The right players are the faculty who teach the underprepared college students in two- and four-year colleges. The right reason is the nationwide problem of underprepared college students, which for decades has been plaguing us in education, industry, and government. One can hardly predict the right time, but one recognizes it when it happens. The track record of Project SYNERGY speaks well for its occurring at the right time. That five hundred or so faculty from forty-one institutions have participated in one or more activities over the last six years is evidence of an enduring collaboration for a common cause.

References

Bloom, B. S., Hastings, J. T., and Madaus, G. F. *Handbook in Formative and Summative Evaluation of Student Learning.* New York: McGraw-Hill, 1971.

Covey, S. R. *The Seven Habits of Highly Effective People.* New York: Simon & Schuster, 1989.

Kotler, L. "Part One: Software Reviews." In Miami-Dade Community College, *Project SYNERGY: Year Three Report,* 1993, pp. 4–5. (ED 392 488)

Miami-Dade Community College. *Project SYNERGY: Software Implementation Report*, 1991. (ED 345 803)
Miami-Dade Community College. *Project SYNERGY: Year Two Report*, 1992. (ED 345 804)
Miami-Dade Community College. *Project SYNERGY: Year Three Report*, 1993. (ED 392 487)
Miami-Dade Community College. *Project SYNERGY: Year Four Report*, 1995. (ED 392 488)

KAMALA ANANDAM is associate dean of educational technologies and director of Project SYNERGY at Miami-Dade Community College, and author of several articles on holistic approaches to teaching and learning and technology.

The faculty and management of Kern Community College District met separately for all-day retreats to discuss faculty loads and compensation in the context of technology integration. The discussions resulted in an acknowledgment of the need for a new approach to faculty compensation and obligations and an exploration of some alternative ways to accomplish that goal.

Faculty Compensation and Obligation: The Necessity of a New Approach Triggered by Technology Integration

Robert D. Allison, David C. Scott

Instructional technology appears to be rapidly gaining momentum today. Computers are used at various levels of intensity in the teaching of virtually all disciplines. Distance education as a mode of delivering instructional programs is growing apace. Use of the Internet, the most recent innovation in providing instruction, is being promoted with great enthusiasm by educators and political leaders alike. Indeed, virtual universities are springing up at a faster rate than the traditional brick-and-mortar types ever did. With all of these new developments, there has been little comment and hardly any in-depth analysis regarding the obligations and compensation of the higher education faculty who are expected to create and implement instructional materials using these technologies. In this chapter, we will review some current practices, present Kern Community College's efforts to change these practices, and suggest some ideas for accomplishing faculty compensation and obligations.

Faculty Compensation

Inadequate compensation frequently has been cited as a barrier to greater faculty interest in adopting new instructional technologies (Olcott and Wright, 1995). Institutions have attempted to address this issue in direct and indirect ways.

Direct Methods. The direct methods include stipends and assigned time. These are the most commonly used methods to compensate faculty for defined responsibilities that are considered to be outside the scope of their usual duties. These activities may include duties such as developing technology-based courses, for example, Internet classes; acting as a team leader in the development of new curriculum; implementing a type of instructional technology; researching the role of technology in the instruction of a particular course or body of knowledge; and assisting other faculty in the application of instructional technology to their disciplines. The assigned time method is used as a substitute for monetary compensation or as an adjunct to it. For longer projects or for continuing duties such as coordinating a program, a certain amount of time can become regularly assigned to a faculty member's duties. Frequently, faculty prefer assigned time to monetary compensation. This is a sensible position. Because we consider regular faculty duties to constitute a full-time job from which we expect outstanding performance, it flies in the face of logic to expect quality work also when demanding responsibilities are added to this job. (Providing additional compensation does not change the fact that the number of hours in a day is fixed.) Extension of the usual ten-month faculty contract into the summer or other off-duty times sometimes is justified on the same basis as assigned time.

Indirect Methods. The indirect ways of addressing this issue include awards and recognition, and staff development. Because some institutions attempt to use these methods, we list them here. They may work well for some faculty for some time but generally will fail as a "compensation" policy unless there is a clear understanding of faculty obligations, discussed in the next section.

Awards and recognition should be part of all institutional practices, but they cannot and should not be thought of as compensation. The need for faculty training often is cited as critical for the success of technological innovations. Some aspects of staff development, particularly providing funds for conference attendance, function as reward mechanisms. Although staff development is indeed necessary and often rewarding in a number of ways, again, it is not compensation.

Faculty Obligations

Faculty obligations are derived from two major sources: what the institution expects of the faculty and what the faculty expect from themselves. When they were students, most of today's faculty experienced a traditional, lecture-based education. Because generally we teach as we have been taught, it is not surprising that the majority of higher education faculty use the lecture as their primary teaching methodology, sometimes accompanying it with various levels of technology, from overhead projectors to multimedia. They see themselves as excellent lecturers and frequently use the lecture method as the standard of excellence against which to compare other methods, often unfavorably. Certainly, the traditional view has the teacher as the central focus of the teaching and learning process. Some faculty do not see any need to adopt "nontraditional" instructional methods. Indeed, they may see these methods as inferior, cost-saving substitutes (or fads), primarily promoted by administrators. Certainly, these faculty do not see themselves as obligated to adopt new technologies in their teaching.

Some institutions may simply expect faculty to be good lecturers. In other cases, faculty may be expected to employ the most effective methods (technological or not), teach at nontraditional times and places, and adjust their teaching and curriculum to the specific needs of their students. How such expectations are communicated include the following:

Job Description or Announcement. A job description clearly sets out the expectations for the position. If a job is being filled with a new person or technology and student needs change, some institutions take the time to reword the expectations in the job description or announcement. Such changes in job descriptions might require additional negotiations in a collective bargaining agreement.

Administrative Communications. Department chairs and other administrators usually convey their expectations to faculty, particularly new faculty. This takes many forms, from beginning-of-the-year pep talks to statements in faculty handbooks to college newsletters.

Evaluations. One of the ways we communicate what is important is through the evaluation process. If we really believe what we are saying, we will evaluate on how well it is being done. Clearly, this must be supported by appropriate understandings between the institution and faculty, including, if applicable, collective bargaining agreements, as well as an institutional culture that supports instructional innovation.

Faculty Contract and Handbook. Most collective bargaining contracts and faculty handbooks include a list of duties and expectations. These may include responsibility for employing technology in teaching and student services.

Institutional Culture. An institutional culture that encourages and supports innovation and tolerates failure is essential if true innovation and experimentation are to take place on a meaningful scale. Administrators must not only talk about their expectations but also provide the support structures necessary for it to occur. No list of faculty duties, contractual language, or even evaluations will work very well without such support.

Changing Expectations

In current practice, then, compensation is based on a traditional model of faculty service. Although faculty generally are expected to engage in curriculum work and program development, in-depth use of technology and the development of nontraditional delivery of instruction usually are considered extra duties and are compensated as such. Faculty obligations are seen in a similar manner by both faculty and administrators.

But it is becoming clear that the role of faculty in higher education is changing. Contrary to some predictions, we do not think the lecture is likely to disappear anytime soon—nor should it. It is a powerful and proven medium and often can be made more effective through the use of technology. For example, the experience at Bakersfield College (a campus of the Kern Community Colleges) has shown large-enrollment lecture classes supplemented with multimedia presentations to be both very effective and popular. However, it is also clear that new technologies and new approaches to instruction are possible and necessary if we are to reach the increasing number of students who require higher education but for various reasons cannot become traditional students.

Based on the writings of leading educators, it is becoming clear that there is increased focus on the role of learning rather than teaching as the operational mind-set in higher education. Terry O'Banion has called for the establishment of "learning colleges," and D. Bruce Johnstone has stated that we must increase "learning productivity" by emphasizing learning while excluding other, less productive student activities (Johnstone, 1992; Barr and Tagg, 1995; O'Banion, 1997). With this emphasis, along with the advent of powerful new tools that can be effectively applied to the learning process, faculty members will be expected to assume a number of roles in addition to or even instead of the traditional one of subject matter expert and transmitter. These roles include curriculum designer, learning facilitator, and technology manager, among others (Beaudoin, 1990; Johnstone, 1992; Barr and Tagg, 1995). Barr and Tagg see faculty as designers of learning methods and environments in which faculty and students work in teams with each other and other staff. Faculty will be responsible for organizing instructional resources so that students will be able to engage in effective independent study and serve as an intermediary between students and available resources (Olcott and Wright, 1995). Thus, it will be necessary for faculty not only to know their subjects well but also to be expert in using technology to design learning environments for their students, some of whom may be many miles away at the time they take the course. Indeed, the concept of the "course" as it is now known may disappear, to be replaced by other learning formats that are not bound in time or place. Just as important, it will be necessary for the faculty member to know which kind of technology—including low technology—is most appropriate for a given instructional situation. To accomplish this, faculty of the future (and of today) should be able to assume the following obligations, some of which already are commonly accepted.

Subject Matter Expert. This is a basic obligation currently and will not change in the future. However, it will become more important not only to know the subject well but also to know how to use technology-based information sources in the subject and tools to keep abreast of developments in the subject.

Faculty currently develop curricula, but they also must be able to design curricula and courses of study to meet specific student needs, which may not be bound by rigid instructional times or places. Curriculum design also should be informed by available instructional technology. Technology generally has been seen as a way to enhance what is taught or to afford different modes of instruction. However, it may be that what is taught also could be affected by the availability of certain technologies. For example, subject matter taught in draft, machine technology, art, and office technology—all have been profoundly changed by the availability of technologies in those subjects.

Courseware Designer. Faculty need to be able to design course materials that can be used in a number of instructional settings and methods, including any one or a combination of the Internet, multimedia, computer-based systems, as well as more traditional modes, such as the lecture and laboratory. This does not mean, however, that faculty must become experts in computer programming, Web page design, or multimedia tool development. Ideally, technical experts and instructional design specialists should be available to provide such services. Faculty should be responsible for pedagogical design and subject matter content, working with the technical consultants as materials are developed.

Instructional Resource Manager. Faculty should be experts in the use of instructional resources in their discipline. Again, they need not be technical experts. However, they must be current in what technologies and pedagogical approaches are available and how they are being used or could be used to help students become more effective learners.

Learning Systems Manager. Community college faculty today might teach a lecture with multimedia, an open entry/open exit laboratory course, an Internet course, a two-way video distance education course, and an independent study course for a few advanced students. Clearly, these individuals must not only be fine traditional teachers but also managers of multiple learning systems. That means they must provide instruction and assistance at a distance, arrange for effective evaluation of student progress, make certain that students receive course materials needed, and manage the whole enterprise.

Staff Developer. The learning curve can be steep when new technology or innovative instructional plans are adopted and initially used. Faculty undertaking such tasks must engage in staff development activities in order to become competent in the use of the tools and new instructional approaches involved. In addition, there should be an expectation that faculty who engage in such pioneering work take responsibility for training and assisting their colleagues in order to increase the rate and extent of these adoptions.

Teacher. Above all, faculty must be effective teachers. But the nature of the traditional obligations as a teacher are changing. The faculty must not only assume the obligations listed but also be prepared to take greater responsibility for student learning, rather than simply give time in the classroom. As costs as well as demand for higher education increase, productivity in the form of greater emphasis on student learning is becoming more important (Johnstone, 1992). Currently, the number of classroom hours is used as the primary basis for determining both student and faculty workload. As we increase our use of technologies like the Internet for the delivery of instruction and base our student evaluations on what students learn at their own pace rather than within a semester or quarter, the nature of faculty assignments and associated obligations may change too. Rather than being required to hold classes for specified periods of time, it may be necessary to assign faculty using other criteria mentioned earlier.

Efforts to Change

Spurred by ongoing union negotiations on faculty load, from 1993 to 1997 the Kern Community College District, both faculty and administration, engaged in a massive, participatory examination of faculty compensation and obligations. The hope was to come up with a loading and duty policy that could be negotiated to meet the needs of the twenty-first century.

The First Retreat. The process began with a faculty-led, all-day load retreat in November 1993. Twenty-five percent of the faculty from the district's three colleges attended. Virtually all of the ten discussion groups initially articulated the need for innovative approaches to compensate faculty for coming up with new instructional delivery approaches and creating learner-oriented environments. As discussions continued, it became evident that the main priority that the faculty wished to emphasize in negotiations was equity of compensation and obligations within the colleges and between faculty of like disciplines across the colleges of the district. Adequate release time for developing new instructional approaches and adequate administrative support in terms of hardware, software, and training were ultimately the only successfully negotiated changes incorporating recognition of the new technology. Many faculty made the point that the California state legislation compensated districts and colleges primarily on the basis of classes built and that this method of compensation was perpetuated by key educational lobby groups in Sacramento, the state capital. One of this chapter's authors attended a national meeting in 1995 at which a well-known East Coast expert on distance learning in higher education expressed the need for new approaches in learner-oriented distance education. But when asked what kind of new approach should be taken for faculty compensation and obligations for those who engaged in such endeavors, that individual replied that the union bargaining agent (of which he was an officer) would not and should not allow for compensation other than that based on the traditional lecture model. The legislative mode of funding based on the lecture model and the union's determination to preserve it for compensation give little or no room for changing faculty obligations and compensation.

The Second Retreat. In September 1994, the management of the Kern Community College District had an all-day faculty load and compensation retreat at which they came up with loading concerns similar to those of the faculty and explored many alternative ways to compensate and encourage faculty for new approaches, primarily release time. There was a tendency on the part of management, however, to emphasize increased productivity; that is, higher conventional class load or more courses per instructor. This was particularly true in the context of the collective bargaining environment. This is yet another barrier to effecting meaningful changes.

We suspect that new approaches advocated in the latter part of this chapter will be challenging to follow through the conventional collective bargaining process, which is usually a beneficial process. Under these circumstances, visionary faculty and administrators would appear to be the only feasible answer to help an institution forge ahead.

New Approaches to Faculty Assignments and Compensation

As faculty roles change, it is reasonable that the basis upon which faculty are compensated changes too. For full-time faculty, this means that the way their "teaching loads" are calculated would be modified. One virtue of the traditional system is that it was easy to calculate faculty load and determine (in a gross manner, anyway) whether faculty were meeting their teaching obligations. Thus, a typical assignment might consist of a given number of hours per week spent in certain defined tasks, such as teaching, counseling and advising, and committee work. But if faculty workloads are to be based on student outcomes rather than number of hours in class and faculty are considered not only teachers but also instructional designers and managers, new criteria must be developed in order to determine what a full-time assignment is. This is not a new idea. Faculty have been given nonteaching duty "release time" for many years. Such assignments sometimes are for short-term projects, but they can also be regular, permanent parts of a faculty assignment.

Questions to Be Answered. The first step in considering differentiated faculty loads must be an agreement on the basic obligations and expectations and on what constitutes additional assignments. Some questions to be answered for basic assignment include the following:

What is the number of instructional units (however calculated) in a full-time teaching assignment?
What other duties are part of the base assignment? If faculty are expected to be courseware designers and learning systems managers, what degree and level of complexity are required as part of the base assignment?
If the subject matter or technology involved in an assignment are particularly challenging, is a greater load credit warranted based on difficulty of preparation for the course design and delivery?
Because faculty often will be working in groups when developing curriculum and courseware and, in many cases, when presenting courses, one person may take primary responsibility for the project. How should the extra effort of the leader be recognized and compensated in the assignment process?

If faculty pioneering early adoption of new technologies have the obligation to train their colleagues, how should their extra effort be recognized and compensated? How should the number of course preparations, sometimes considered part of load formulas now, be treated as expectations of faculty broaden?

The greater the number of sites for distance education, the greater the complexity and time required for instructional management, both during and outside of class time. How should the number of sites be treated in faculty compensation and expectations?

A large number of students in a distance education course will require increased time on the part of the faculty to correspond to student e-mail messages and participate in electronic chat rooms. How should this time be configured into the new approach?

Units of success are likely to become part of the new approach. They are defined by the college as an instructional workload standard that calls for the delivery and evaluation of instruction to a given number of students and the accomplishment of a set of predetermined instructional outcomes. Barr and Tagg even suggest using a productivity measure defined as "cost per unit of learning per student" (Barr and Tagg, 1995, p. 17). Even though this suggestion might be controversial, it does question the need for a particular number of class hours for all students to achieve success. What should be the role of this concept in the new approach?

If the faculty member has responsibility for physical resources at a level which requires coordination or management duties in excess of that normally expected, how should assignment credit be awarded?

Should types of assignment be considered in compensation?

Traditional teaching is unlikely to disappear anytime soon. Some faculty may be better suited to such teaching or simply prefer it. If, as a result, those faculty are given less responsibility in areas such as curriculum design and instructional management, their teaching assignments might be adjusted to compensate for this. Similarly, other faculty might have greater responsibility in, for example, instructional technology applications to their disciplines and have smaller teaching loads.

Other Suggestions. We do not suggest that determining faculty assignments using these or other criteria would be an easy matter, but we believe that it can be done and indeed must be done if we are to take full advantage of the potential of new technologies. It will require considerable judgment, trust, and good will among all concerned. To achieve optimum equity, it would be well to define in advance a "catalogue" of project and assignment types and associated levels of difficulty. In addition, we suggest that the number of students beyond particular thresholds be defined in order to determine load levels.

Institutional Obligations

Just as the faculty have new obligations to their students, the institution must provide the support necessary for faculty to meet those obligations. In other words, the institution itself has obligations too, both to faculty and to students. Indeed, support in the form of compensation, reassigned time, staff development, and equipment availability frequently have been cited as barriers to the implementation of technology (Beaudoin, 1990; Hammond and others, 1992; Olcott and Wright, 1995; Albright, 1996).

Tools and Maintenance. We cannot expect faculty to provide state-of-the-art technology-based instruction if they and their students are not provided with appropriate equipment and software. Such items include individual faculty workstations, development and training laboratory facilities, an adequate number of student workstations, distance learning facilities, current software releases and updates, and other technology as needed. The institution must commit the funding necessary for the acquisition, maintenance, support, and upgrading of these technologies.

Support Personnel and Related Resources. Support personnel include instructional designers, trainers, programmers and analysts, software and hardware maintenance personnel, video engineers and technicians, Web "masters," and other technical and support staff required for an effective operation.

Training and Retraining. Faculty would be more interested in instructional technology if training were provided, even for younger faculty who might be expected to have a greater level of computer literacy or at least familiarity. Higher education faculty are well-versed in their disciplines but very few have had a background in instructional technology (high or low). Technologies change quickly, so it will be necessary to follow training with retraining on a regular basis. Thus, the establishment and maintenance of a regular training program is essential.

We suggest that a summer seminar on instructional technology and the community college student be given to all new faculty and be made available for senior faculty who require updating their technological skills. The seminar could include specific instruction on the use of the technology available at the particular college and give the faculty members time to develop materials in their disciplines. It would be desirable in some cases for specific discipline areas to offer such workshops for their own faculty in order to promote the change process.

Assigned Time and Stipends. Institutions are obligated to provide adequate and realistic compensation for the work performed by faculty that is over and above their normally assigned duties. This can be in the form of stipends and other types of monetary compensation, assigned (release) time, and paid time beyond the contract year.

Clear Expectations. As faculty assignments become more extensive and complex, it will be more critical than ever before to work with faculty and develop clear job descriptions and performance expectations.

Trust. Finally, if teaching assignments are to be based more on student outcomes and less on the number of hours an instructor is in a classroom, then the institution and its administrators must trust their faculty's professionalism.

Summary

Current practices regarding faculty compensation and obligations are based on a traditional model of higher education. That model sees faculty instructional duties in terms of a given number of teaching ("contact") hours or units per week, term, or year. Innovative approaches may be encouraged but are generally seen as additional duties and are compensated as such. Rarely are they included as part of the fundamental obligation of faculty.

This chapter suggested a new approach that assumes an expanded faculty role. This role would include both traditional and new obligations: subject matter expert, curriculum developer and designer, courseware designer, instructional resource manager, and learning systems manager. And of course, faculty would remain responsible for their own professional development. This would necessitate a new approach to compensation, one that would be based primarily on student learning rather than hours in a classroom. It also would require the recognition of institutional obligations for current tools, support personnel and related resources, training and retraining, reassigned time and stipends for faculty, clear expectations, and trust in faculty professionalism.

Through mutual trust and respect, faculty and administrators can establish a new approach to defining institutional expectations, faculty compensation, and faculty obligations in a technology-rich teaching and learning environment.

References

Albright, M. J. "Instructional Technology and Higher Education: Rewards, Rights, and Responsibilities." Keynote address presented to the Southern Regional Faculty and Instructional Development Consortium, Baton Rouge, La., Feb. 5, 1996. (ED 392 412)

Barr, R. B., and Tagg, J. "From Teaching to Learning: A New Paradigm for Undergraduate Education." *Change,* 1995, 27 (6), 13–25.

Beaudoin, M. "The Instructor's Changing Role in Distance Education." *American Journal of Distance Education,* 1990, 4 (2), 21–29.

Hammond, N., Gardener, N., Heath, S., Kibby, M., Mayes, T., McAleese, R., Mullings, C., and Trapp, A. "Blocks to the Use of Information Technology in Higher Education." *Computers and Education,* 1992, 18 (1), 155–162.

Johnstone, D. B. "Learning Productivity: A New Imperative for American Higher Education." Edited version of a monograph published by the State University of New York as part of a series, Studies in Public Higher Education, 1992. [http://www.educom.edu/program/hlii/articles/johnstone.html]

O'Banion, T. *A Learning College for the Twenty-First Century.* Annapolis Junction, Md.: Community College Press, 1997. (ED 409 042)

Olcott, D., and Wright, S. J. "An Institutional Support Framework for Increasing Faculty Participation in Postsecondary Distance Education." *American Journal of Distance Education,* 1995, 9 (3), 5–17.

ROBERT D. ALLISON *is interim president at Bakersfield College.*

DAVID C. SCOTT *is emeritus assistant chancellor for personnel at Kern Community College District.*

This chapter argues the need for college planners to prepare for serious competition from for-profit providers by assessing the market niches in which their institutions can successfully compete. The strengths of community colleges lie in their ability to provide learning support services for learners in their local communities.

What Are Community Colleges to Do When Disney and Microsoft Enter the Higher Education and Training Market?

Don Doucette

Although the emergence of private competition in the higher education market has been predicted for some time (most explicitly by Davis and Botkin, 1994), the assertion that Microsoft, Disney, and other corporations that are not in the field of higher education might actually contend for that market has, until recently, been dismissed as either hyperbole or fear-mongering. However, as the future becomes present and its shape becomes ever clearer, the idea that colleges and universities might actually have to compete with the likes of Disney and Microsoft for paying customers (students) has become a more realistic and urgent concern. The emerging fundamental planning questions facing all institutions of higher education are as unfamiliar to most educators as the boardrooms of corporate America are to a layperson. What are we as public or private institutions going to do? What are we to become? What business will we be in? In which market niches can we compete when Michael Eisner, Bill Gates, Robert Allen, Ted Turner, Rupert Murdoch, John McGraw, and others like them in the future become, in effect, college presidents—CEOs of multinational information, communications, and educational providers?

Of course, it is not possible to demonstrate Disney's and Microsoft's dominance in the higher education market. As of this writing, Disney's ventures into higher education have been largely limited to courses offered to visitors to its theme parks. Microsoft's postsecondary training activities have been confined to training that supports its own software products. Nevertheless, it is important for college planners and leaders to acknowledge that

NEW DIRECTIONS FOR COMMUNITY COLLEGES, no. 101, Spring 1998 © Jossey-Bass Publishers enough technological, economic, and social forces are converging and leading directly to some version of this competitive future to make it an uncertain one. Even those who are not convinced that Disney and Microsoft are serious threats to their jobs tend to agree that increasing private competition portends change—business not as usual—for their colleges and universities. Also growing is the recognition that the change that is looming for these institutions will be shaped and motivated by forces previously unfamiliar to higher education planners, that is, by market forces of supply and demand, customer choice and satisfaction, product positioning, and market niche.

This chapter assumes that serious competition for higher education and training dollars will come from the private sector. The argument will be made that those colleges and universities that explicitly acknowledge this competition in their planning and that position themselves to compete successfully in one or more market niches that play to their institutional strengths have a good chance of surviving, even prospering.

Exploding Demand for Higher Education and Training

The marketplace dynamics at work are not hard to identify. One of the most dramatic and obvious trends in the workplace is the increasing demand for new and higher skill levels. This demand is not coming only from adult workers who continually face pressure to upgrade their skills but also from new entrants into the workforce. For the latter group, a high school diploma is insufficient qualification for a good job. Whether or not an institution accepts this demand as real and includes the education and training of adult workers as its principal mission, the fact remain that upwards of 75 percent of the existing workforce will require training in the next five years. When new jobs requiring at least two years of college are created, it leads to a high-demand market for higher education, primarily technical training among an increasingly diverse student body.

Although there remains a substantial number of eighteen-year-olds who want a full-time, sequential, residential college education, older and nontraditional students have outnumbered these traditional students for nearly a decade. These older students have different demands and require different strategies, programs, and services from the colleges that serve them. Primarily, adult students want convenience. They are sensitive to cost, but they are even more sensitive to issues of time, place, length of commitment, and other aspects of access. What many adult students want is "anytime, anyplace" education and training, and many appear willing to pay for it.

In this environment—where the potential for making a lot of money by delivering education and training to an expanding market of adults exists alongside an increasingly price-sensitive market of more traditional-age students—there is really no doubt that someone in the private, public, nonprofit, or for-profit sectors will find ways to deliver the needed education and training in more effective, efficient, and student-centered ways. Now that the cost of a traditional higher education has reached up to $1,000 per week in some colleges—or about $100 a lecture—the demand for market-driven higher education will be undeniable.

The Developing Infrastructure for Delivery of Education and Training. The infrastructure for video on demand is already being built, the solutions to technical problems await only sorting out the winners among competing technologies and establishing commercial viability for selected solutions. Murder investigators (at least those on television) have a standard explanation: "Follow the money." Following the money leads to the inevitable conclusion that companies such as Microsoft and Disney will become major providers of higher education and training as soon as the technology required to deliver content becomes affordable to sufficiently large markets—first to video arcades, and then to businesses and homes, in that order. Although skepticism abounds, no one really believes that the last hundred-foot gap of wire from the street to the home will not be bridged, if not by cable, telephone, or utility companies, then by wireless providers. Nor can we count on the technophobia of the average American to avoid buying and using the $500 television that is really a computer hooked to the global information network. Prototypes, such as Web TV, are already in the electronics stores in the local mall. As soon as this device can be easily used by an ordinary individual with a remote control, the education and training revolution begins! Estimates of the size of this market range from $100 billion to $400 billion. Colleges and universities as we know them are hardly immune from such enormous market pressures.

Nor will all of the competition come from the for-profit sector. One might even argue that Disney and Microsoft have bigger fish to fry than higher education. However, the Western Governors University—a private, nonprofit, virtual university sponsored by the governors of eighteen Western states—this academic year will issue its first Request for Proposals for providers of the content, assessment methodologies, and courses that it will broker and then credential with degrees. Competition for the higher education market is not a prediction of the future. It is a present reality that responds directly to marketplace forces of product, price, place, and promotion.

College planners simply must acknowledge and accommodate this competition as they consider the market niches in which their institutions have a fair chance of competing successfully. College planning needs to think in market terms that consider specifically the economic forces and technologies that have the most profound impact on the traditional model of higher education.

Economics of Technology in the University. Much has been written on future scenarios for higher education, but one of the most cogent and applicable to this argument was published in *Science* magazine in an article entitled "Electronics and the Dim Future of the University" (Noam, 1995). Eli Noam, dean of the Graduate College of Economics and Communications at Columbia University, offers an analysis that is useful as the basis for examining market niche in the increasingly competitive business of higher education.

Noam dissects the role of the university to show that it consists of three elements: (1) the creation of knowledge and evaluation of its validity; (2) the preservation of information; and (3) the transmission of this information to others. Accomplishing each of these functions is based on a set of technologies and economics that together with history give rise to institutions that in the modern era we have known as universities. However, Noam points out that "change the technology and economics, and the institutions must change, eventually" (p. 247).

Since the royal library in Nineveh in Assyria and the Great Library of Alexandria, the model of centrally stored information has defined our model of higher education. Noam writes, "Scholars came to information storage institutions and produced collaboratively still more information there, and students came to the scholars." What modern information technology has done is to reverse the flow of information. "In the past people came to information, which was stored at the university. In the future, the information will come to people, wherever they are" (p. 249). Because information technology allows the decentralization and distribution of vast stores of information and the creation of virtual communities, the advantages of the physical proximity of scholars to each other and to information are greatly reduced. These same technologies and economics are rendering the university's function of storing information obsolete—certainly breaking its exclusive hold as repository of knowledge.

The third function of the university, transmitting information, its teaching role, is under great stress in the university, for student-teacher interaction comes with a big price tag. Noam notes that "If alternative instructional technologies and credentialing systems can be devised, there will be a migration away from classic campus-based higher education. While it is true that the advantages of electronic forms of instruction have sometimes been absurdly exaggerated, the point is not that they are superior to face-to-face teaching (though the latter is often romanticized), but that they can be provided at dramatically lower cost" (p. 251). Noam also agrees that the ultimate providers of electronic-based curricula will not be universities but commercial entities.

Noam acknowledges that by presenting a bleak future for the university, he is inviting a response that reaffirms the importance of quality education, academic values, and the historic role of education in personal growth, but this is beside the point. "The question is not whether universities are important to society, to knowledge, or to members—they are—but rather whether the economic foundation of the present system can be maintained and sustained in the face of the changed flow of information brought about by electronic communications." He continues: "To be culturally important is necessary but, unfortunately, not sufficient for a major claim on public and private resources. We may regret this, but we can't deny it" (Noam, 1995, p. 253).

Institutional Scenarios

Noam's analysis can be used to predict the prospects for different types of institutions. The negative impacts of the changing technology and economics of higher education will not be uniform. Colleges will fare better or worse depending upon type, curriculum, admission standards, and cost—all of which determine their market niche. In general, the most negative effects of information technology will be on mass undergraduate and nonselective professional and graduate education and, consequently, upon those institutions that depend on these missions for a substantial amount of their revenues or for justification for public support.

Research Universities. Electronic communications will be a mixed blessing for research universities. The explosion of information and its distribution will make the research and knowledge validation function more important than ever. This is the good news. More problematic will be maintaining universities as physical islands of research, because physical proximity of scholars may become less important. To the extent that aspiring scholars follow and seek to locate in physical proximity to scholarly activity, the teaching function of the research university may be maintained as an outgrowth of the research function for the few select and specialized students who will be asked to pay much higher costs for the privilege of being taught by noted scholars. Diminishing the university's role in mass undergraduate education will have profound and disruptive effects on these generally quite large institutions with massive existing infrastructures. For, as we know, the large lecture has often subsidized the full research professor.

Liberal Arts Colleges. The prospects for liberal arts colleges and other small colleges are somewhat dicier. Having no appreciable research and knowledge validation function, these institutions have always depended on very high-quality teaching as their reason for being. Much like the elite universities, only those liberal arts and small colleges that are able to provide a high-quality education experience for a dedicated constituency that can support the very high cost of doing so will thrive.

In fact, since true teaching and learning is about much more than the transmission of information but rather about mentoring, internalization, role models, guidance, socialization, interaction, and group activity, in many ways the liberal arts college is precisely suited to provide the quality of interaction, the value-added "high touch" counterpart to "high tech" transmission of information that most of us believe represents quality higher education. However, this quality is likely to be limited to those who can afford it or who have the benefit of private sponsorship. Only those colleges that can successfully appeal to a specific market niche of cities or special-interest students and financial backers (such as religious denominations, corporations, or professional associations) are likely to prosper.

Regional and Nonselective Colleges and Universities. Because the most negative impacts of electronic communications will be on mass undergraduate and professional education, nonselective universities that traditionally serve this market niche have the most precarious prospects. If degrees can be earned at home or in extension centers, regional universities will be forced to make a persuasive case to prospective students that they will be better off by moving out to the country—where last century's best thinkers ingeniously thought to locate them.

However, without access to the scholars of the research university and without the benefit of the small size of the liberal arts college, these universities will become marginal in meeting the needs of higher education's current student base. Their costs will rise so that they will not enjoy a price advantage over electronically delivered degrees. Only those regional universities that differentiate their mission and specialize in areas of great concern to sponsoring entities (such as state governments) will have sufficient call on resources to survive in their current form.

Community Colleges. The prospects for community colleges are mixed. On the one hand, because they currently perform the mass undergraduate education function that is most under pressure from electronically mediated alternatives and for-profit providers, their hold on the adult worker market will be significantly weakened, presenting a major threat to institutional viability. However, the high-quality technical education and training mission of community colleges will prosper. Least affected by electronic forms of higher education will be skills training that requires hands-on instruction and feedback, which comprehensive community colleges have a long history of providing.

Community colleges have also been on the forefront of experimenting with technology and other alternative delivery systems to accommodate the schedules of nontraditional students. However, although these efforts may buy community colleges time, it would be foolish to think that community colleges will ever be able to compete successfully with Microsoft and Disney in disseminating high-quality and convenient higher education and training content in electronically mediated form. In the mass undergraduate higher education market, community colleges will lose any head-to-head competition with these corporate giants.

The Community College Niche

So, we return to the original question: What are community colleges to do when Microsoft and Disney can deliver Introduction to Biological Concepts and College Algebra to your living room, courses taught by renowned and entertaining scholars and produced by the best that Disney has to offer?

Community colleges have the option of focusing on their occupational education and technical training mission where they have strong market advantages. In fact, some state legislatures would support community colleges narrowing their focus on this function, which is highly valued as supporting states' economic development activity. However, abandoning their general education and transfer functions is appropriately anathema to most community college professionals, and this option is unlikely to be pursued. On the other side of the coin, community colleges could opt to focus solely on general education, becoming in effect the poor person's liberal arts college, or solely on developmental education. However, neither of these options is likely or sustainable. One of the few realistic options for community colleges is to find and optimize a market niche that plays to their strengths.

Community colleges must acknowledge what they do well, perhaps better than any other institutions of higher education save selective liberal arts colleges. Community colleges have a long-standing commitment to and know how to support learners. The principal clientele of community colleges—nonselective students and students who cannot move out of the area—have little access to selective liberal arts colleges or other environments that nurture small communities of learners. However, these same students are arguably most in need of learning assistance. Many, maybe most, community college students need learning support, guidance, organization, skills development, and a variety of other support services. Some of these students will be able to afford to enroll in courses offered pay-per-view at home or work, but many will need support in order to benefit from these courses, and such support is likely only to be available through local community colleges.

Rather than competing with Microsoft and Disney, community colleges will prosper if they do what they do best: provide learning support services to help students learn, regardless of where they get their information. In some cases, community colleges may become brokers of content supplied by for-profit providers, wrapping a learning support environment around the content that students receive in their homes or businesses. Or community colleges may simply become learning support centers, institutions that are skilled in supporting learners who get information from a variety of sources, including from the community college itself.

In other words, the community colleges that will survive the frontal assault waged on their comprehensive mission by information-age higher education providers will be those who understand their niche as becoming what Terry O'Banion (1997) has dubbed "learning colleges." They will shed their role as mere disseminators of information in favor of the role of supporters of learning. They will draw upon years of experience in student development, student support services, and developmental education to become the best learning support organizations in the world. Disney and Microsoft cannot compete in the provision of these services in support of student learning. In their local communities, this is the strategic market niche for community colleges.

The Community College as Learning College. O'Banion (1997) defines and articulates the principles of what is certainly one of the most viable options for community colleges to pursue in light of private competition for their current higher education market. "The learning college places learning first and provides educational experiences for learners anyway, anywhere, anytime" (p. 47). It assumes that educational experiences are designed for the convenience of learners, rather than for the convenience of institutions and their faculty and staff. The assumption is that education is designed to optimize learning, which most fundamentally occurs by doing, not by sitting and listening. O'Banion also helps to answer key questions of substance, organization, and staffing that must be answered if community colleges are to get any closer to understanding the market niche ideally suited for them in the coming era of video on demand.

Functions. First and foremost, learning colleges will become warehouses of learning options and experiences, learning support services, and expertise. They will provide access to self-paced instructional materials, expert interactive learning systems, tutoring services, collaborative learning options, service learning projects, catalogues of information and links, access to the World Wide Web, reading programs, community forums, assessment services, field trips, commercial software, and video services—any conceivable learning option on every conceivable topic at multiple levels of competency and skill. The principal function of the learning college will be to collect, catalogue, and inventory such learning experiences, and to guide and support students in their use.

Facilities. Learning colleges will benefit from a consolidation of learning resources, libraries, computer labs and networks, video and telecommunications resources, learning assistance and tutoring centers, student development and student services. There are community colleges that are already moving to build facilities that consolidate information resources. However, a learning college will be based not so much on the consolidation of information services as on the consolidation and colocation of learning support services with them.

Roles. The roles of faculty and staff in learning colleges will be defined in terms of the needs of learners, and these roles are likely to become more differentiated and specialized, drawing on the strengths and preferences of college faculty and staff. Some will undoubtedly do exactly what they do now. Good lecturers will still lecture. Effective counselors will still counsel. Talented discussion leaders will still lead discussions. Overwhelmingly, however, most faculty and staff will be engaged in a variety of activities in support of learning and learners. Some will encourage and facilitate enrollment, some will help form learning cohorts, and some will assess learner needs, abilities, interests, and learning styles. Others will provide content expertise and technical assistance; still others will create standards and outcome measures. Some will arrange field trips, internships, and service learning opportunities, while others nurture interpersonal relationships, guide, tutor, coach, and mentor. Finally, some may simply broker services from other educational providers. Although it is impossible to define exactly what community colleges that support learners in their communities will look and operate like, it is clear what functions will take place in these environments—functions that Microsoft and Disney are unlikely to be able to deliver to the local communities.

Strategies for College Administrators. It is certainly easier to suggest that community colleges become learning colleges than it is to specify a course of action. In truth, the circumstances and idiosyncratic cultures of most colleges and universities make generalizing about implementation strategies dangerous and silly. O'Banion (1997) offers a number of practical suggestions for helping community colleges move toward the goal of becoming a learning college. These include the strategy of capitalizing on "triggering events," supporting innovation across the board, and attempting to link innovative practices into more cohesive institutional development initiatives. He also provides specific examples of the efforts being made by a number of leading community colleges to put the learner first, though these also demonstrate the variety of approaches that are possible.

However, some generalizations can be made about strategies that all colleges can benefit from. First and foremost, college planners must accept that they are involved in the business of higher education. As difficult as this is for most educators to swallow, it is important to understand and plan for an appropriate niche in the higher education and training market. Then, community colleges that are serious about preparing for a future defined by commercial on-demand video can do the following things: (1) build the necessary network infrastructure to allow voice, video, and data communications with homes and workplaces; (2) develop expertise among all faculty and staff to support adult learners, including focusing professional development programs on advances made in learning theory and cognitive science in the past decade; (3) reorganize and integrate their information resource centers and libraries, learning assistance centers, professional development programs, assistive technologies, computer networks, and information systems to develop world-class learning support resources; (4) reorganize their curriculum and assessment methodologies to support outcomes-based credentialing of students' knowledge and skills; (5) support faculty and staff in their efforts to develop multiple learning options for students, including self-paced instruction, learning communities, collaborative learning, activity-based learning, and various forms of asynchronous learning; and finally (6) change administrative structures and practices that are obstacles to putting the student first—that is, actively dismantle business as usual. All colleges can productively pursue these strategies to create more flexible colleges that are more focused on student needs. All that achieve some success toward this basic goal will likely survive, even flourish, in the face of increased competition.

It is ironic that a business analysis of the strengths and likely niche for community colleges in the emerging free and fiercely competitive higher education market recommends a course of action that is a long-held dream of many of the founders of the modern community college. Student development professionals have long held up the learning college as an ideal to strive for. Instead, it is market forces that are pushing community colleges to fulfill its destiny: to make universal access to lifelong learning meaningful.

References

Davis, S., and Botkin, J. *The Monster Under the Bed.* New York: Simon & Schuster, 1994.
Noam, E. "Electronics and the Dim Future of the University." *Science,* Oct. 13, 1995.
O'Banion, T. *The Learning College.* Phoenix: American Council on Education and Oryx Press, 1997.

DON DOUCETTE serves the Metropolitan Community Colleges, Kansas City, Missouri, as vice chancellor for education and technology. He previously served as associate director of the League for Innovation in the Community College, and in various positions at Johnson County Community College and the Maricopa Community Colleges.

The significant aspects and processes involved in integrating technology into education as explained in the previous nine chapters are synthesized in this chapter and presented as a call for action.

A Call for Action

Kamala Anandam

Time and again, history has shown us that when groups of individuals exert persistent and concerted effort to achieve their goals, they do indeed succeed. As educators, we need to do the same now to use technology as our greatest ally in providing an accessible, affordable, quality teaching and learning environment for our students. By way of setting the stage for this effort, this chapter offers the following call for action for your consideration. This list has emerged from the ideas presented in the various chapters of this volume.

When it comes to technology integration with teaching and learning, subscribe to the slogan "It is not a question of competence but a question of cultural change" so that your attention will be directed toward human processes and organizational structures.

Take sufficient time—a year maybe—and involve faculty, staff, and students to create a vision for the future and to identify the milestones for progress in the use of technology as your greatest ally in achieving your vision.

Rather than wait for sufficient funds to be available all at once to do everything your college wishes to do with technology, conceptualize the "bigger picture" and seize every opportunity to paint a piece of that picture.

Focus on the top twenty-five enrollment courses for investment in technology in order to get the "biggest bang for the buck."

Provide ongoing, discipline-based faculty and staff development in order to achieve enduring practices of technology integration.

Facilitate an institutionwide plan to review and enhance curriculum programs with technology in mind so that you can offer greater and more complex content in ways that were not possible before.

Consider the Project SYNERGY Integrator (PSI) as a tool colleges can use to direct the attention of publishers to producing quality instructional software and to help them achieve a critical mass through PSI.

Contribute your institution's fair share to the common bank of intellectual resources.

See your institution as it never was, think "outside the box," and ask, "Why not?"

KAMALA ANANDAM *is associate dean of educational technologies and director of Project SYNERGY at Miami-Dade Community College.*

This chapter reviews additional literature and explores themes related to implementing new technologies on campus.

Sources and Information: Identifying and Implementing Technologies for Higher Education

Janel Ann Soulé Henriksen

The use of information technology within academia has quickly become a benchmark by which academic institutions define their competitiveness and effectiveness as centers for learning. This issue of *New Directions for Community Colleges* has presented a comprehensive review of the policies, organizational cultures, and pedagogical issues that either hasten or hinder the adoption of new technologies designed to make instruction and operations more effective and efficient. This chapter explores additional issues and themes.

Planning for Implementation: Considering Organizational Culture

Redesigning curricula or making changes in delivery of instruction cannot be considered without first understanding the existing culture of the organization in the midst of significant change. Several articles have addressed the challenges that community colleges must confront in order to create an effective plan to implement new technologies within academic and administrative services.[1]

Reacting to Technological Change. In "Educational Technology and Transformation," Gilbert (1995) identifies common institutional reactions to significant change in the uses of technology. Such reactions affect both the organizational culture and the structure of academic and administrative communities. First, as faculty members become more aware that traditional

91

methods of teaching may not be as effective as they once were, they report that their teaching methods are improved by the use of information technology. Second, as more systems and services are implemented, fewer staff and faculty members are prepared to maintain, support, and provide training for these systems. Although most colleges have acquired Internet access, they cannot yet identify the extent to which faculty and staff use computer technology for academic purposes. Third, colleges and universities have not consistently reconfigured their accounting systems to recognize the "unusual nature of annual computer-related expenses" (p. 17). Citing the American Association for Higher Education's (AAHE) Teaching, Learning and Technology roundtable programs, Gilbert recommends that community colleges adopt an approach to coordinating technological changes on campus, and he describes the materials available from AAHE that can encourage exchanges of information among campuses.

Johnson and Lobello (1996) also offer reflections on the impact of technology on the culture of the community college. Their three-part monograph includes a series of essays that reflect the views of a number of community college leaders on the role of technology and on strategies for responding to change.

Maintaining Mission. A burgeoning information culture can have a profound impact on perceptions about mission, according to Paine (1996). He suggests that colleges should retain a focus on student learning while at the same time providing invaluable information as their reach expands with advanced uses of technology.

Constructing the Campus. The physical setting of a community college, and the way people within the organization feel about it, may influence the implementation of technology. Biehle (1996) writes in "What Are the Urgent Design Projects?" that priorities for campus building projects are changing rapidly. Thirty-five senior campus officials in the St. Louis area, nine of whom were from community colleges, were surveyed regarding their priorities for construction on their respective campuses. Almost half of all the participants believed that the integration of new technology on campus, "from classrooms and offices to distance learning facilities," was the primary focus of new campus construction projects (pp. 23–24). Biehle also noted that there was a great deal of ambivalence about how best to incorporate the emerging new technologies. There was skepticism about the benefits and concern about the scope of the changes that were to come. Some of the administrators surveyed noted that wiring needs were influencing the design of all facilities on campus. As one participant stated, "a library will never be a library again" (p. 24).

Changing Organizational Structures: Creating the Learning College. In "The Role of the Community College Chair in Organizational Change" (1996), Mellow appropriately notes that the typical community college organization resides in what she calls the "Late Industrial Era." She recommends that for a college to grow and adapt, changes must be made to traditional organizational structures that may be too rigid to allow for the effective use of new technologies and information. She suggests that using the concept of the college as a "learning organization" is one way to make the existing institutional culture more receptive to change.

O'Banion (1997) describes the learning college model for community colleges. He discusses the pressures that may work to resist change, and reviews the origins in earlier education reform movements of the current emphasis on learning. The design of educational experiences that focus on helping students to make passionate connections to learning necessarily involves openness to innovations in technology.

Planning Strategically. An additional source of information on how colleges can confront issues and challenges to their efforts to implement information technology comes from Baltzer (1994). In "The Learning Action Plan: A New Approach to Information Technology Planning in Community Colleges," Baltzer has created a resource for those who are directly responsible for planning, managing, and supporting information technology in two-year colleges. She offers a strategic planning model called the Learning Action Plan. Based on work conducted in the ten-campus Maricopa County Community College District, the plan "focuses on what the IT organization must do to remain a vital and contributing part of the overall institution" (p. 2). An understanding of and appreciation for an organization's culture is essential to planning. Not only will strategies for implementing technology differ on the basis of an institution's culture, but a change in the organizational culture of a college may also be necessary to "ensure the survival and long-term effectiveness of the IT organization" (p. 3). In her research, Baltzer covers many key areas, including identifying organizational culture, customer communities, and the current technology level of the organization; defining key organizational goals; developing and communicating a shared vision; and developing processes for continuous feedback for long-term planning.

Implementing Technology

How should an administrator accustomed to "traditional" teaching and learning methodologies respond when faced with the task of understanding and evaluating the new technological tools available to meet the needs of the college's faculty and staff?

Introducing the Internet. For the novice administrator who is stalled in the slow lane on the information superhighway, Brumbaugh and McRae (1995) have prepared "An Internet Primer for Community College Administrators." It provides a basic introduction to the Internet, including its history and current uses, definitions of key terminology, and discussion of many potentially time-saving and cost-effective tools for educators.

Managing Resources. McCabe (1996) describes the relationship between education and resource management. Using an economic model of developing distance learning, he examines the community college mission and its place in the educational community. In stressing the necessity of adequate funding, he explores the history and future of the institutional advancement process, including building assets through the use of fundraising teams and effective leadership.

Assessing Effectiveness. In "Attitudes of Community College Faculty and Students Towards the Use of Videodisc Technology in the Classroom," Olson, Muyskens, and Busby (1995) present the results of a study of the use of videodisc technology in classrooms at a campus in the Dallas Community College District. Such a study can serve as a model for assessing the effectiveness of new teaching methods or administrative practices. Students and faculty were surveyed to gauge their perceptions regarding the use of interactive videodiscs in classroom settings. Both students and faculty who had observed this technology were impressed with it and preferred the use of videodiscs to the more traditional use of slides.

Developing Personnel. LeDuc (1996) provides a thoughtful analysis of how best to develop the technical skills and talents of end users who need to be secure in their use of programs and software for business purposes. "Personnel Development: Key to Organizational Strength" reviews methods that may encourage staff members to use new technology. LeDuc enumerates easy steps to help an organization refocus its energies with regard to technology. He suggests ways to create opportunities for technical training within the context of a staff member's existing job responsibilities through special assignments, conferences, and continual evaluation and counseling. The author is also careful to illustrate current barriers to such professional development, and states that today's organizational climate is frequently too negative to be receptive to change. Organizational health is an issue that should be confronted by administrators who seek to implement positive changes within their colleges, and LeDuc reminds us that "organizations have a vested interest in actively promoting professional development" (p. 10).

Orienting Students to Computers. A number of troubling issues swirl around the question of access to technology. Does a campus that increasingly relies on e-mail interaction between students and faculty create a new underclass of students who are the technological have-nots? Because many community college students may not have computers of their own, their access to information technology may be limited to what is available for use on campus. Similarly, students attending community college in an economically depressed area may be at a disadvantage because the college they attend may not be able to keep pace with the high costs of technology (Gilbert, 1996).

Reed (1996) addresses this issue by presenting exercises that professors may use to orient students to computers even while a college may be waiting for grant money to expand their labs or establish the college's computer network. In "The Silicon Ceiling: Technology, Literacy and the Community College Student," Reed describes writing classes that link students to networks through which they critique and comment upon one another's work, with the idea that this will certainly "help students gain a sense of entitlement, familiarity, and cognitive resonance with the 'electronic conversation'" (p. 1). The advantage of computer-mediated writing classes is that the format is democratic and includes all students in the class experience.

Computerizing Administrative Systems and Services. Effective implementation of new software applications for use in administrative systems and services at community colleges presents another kind of challenge. Frequently, state and federal mandates cause college and university officials to reevaluate the quality and effectiveness of their current financial and accounting systems. Applebaum and colleagues (1995) describe the process by which eight community colleges in Florida formed a consortium that helped these campuses come into full compliance with legal mandates. The eight campuses collaborated to develop four applications required of them by the state of Florida and the federal government: financial management, student information, personnel and payroll, and facilities. "Business Process Reengineering: A Consortium Approach with End Users as the Architect Produces Dramatic Results" explains the process by which these eight colleges organized their consortium, defined their objectives, and arrived at strategies for success. The consortium members recognized the benefits of pooling their resources to meet state database requirements, thereby providing long-term solutions to ongoing needs. The colleges developed a nineteen-step process by which they could identify necessary technologies and implement the most appropriate and cost-effective software.

Maricopa County Community College District (MCCCD) in Arizona faced similar challenges to the effective implementation of new administrative computing systems using client/server architecture. Schroeder and Bleed (1996) wrote in "Apollo: Changing the Way We Work" about the process of obtaining feedback from more than three hundred employees as part of the process of finding a company that could introduce new practices and evaluate existing ones. MCCCD contracted with Oracle Corporation and with the cooperation of Axiom Business Consultants created the new Learning Center System. This article describes the context, design, and implementation of this visionary project.

Measuring the Quality of Technological Support Services. To effectively incorporate new technologies, and to ensure that systems are used appropriately, it is critical that end users have access to customer assistance staff who are knowledgeable about information technology systems on campus. Portland Community College was experiencing a noticeable decline in the quality of customer service within the information technology division, and morale in that department was low. "Customer Services at Portland Community College—Then and Now," by Eaton and Grant (1996), describes the importance of recognizing the need to reevaluate the way customer assistance is delivered to faculty and staff when new technologies are introduced. Steps to improve trust and morale within the customer service team were implemented, training for staff members became a new priority, and staff members were given the skills and decision-making authority to meet customers' needs. Customer expectations were managed better and the department found new ways to measure the quality of technological support services.

Implications of Technology Implementation

The hope is that the implementation of information technology will resolve a myriad of conflicts and problems inherent in institutions of higher education, but technology integration can also create serious staffing and financial woes.

Drawbacks of Outsourcing. Community colleges may discover that their employees lack the technical skills to manage new software and hardware. Frequently the task of managing systems and services is outsourced to private contractors. Although this option is typically cost-effective for a college, it raises concern over the blurred boundary between education and business. Educators may feel that an overemphasis on "hi-tech" makes their institutions mere marketplace competitors rather than bastions of higher learning. Also, employee morale and the sense of campus community may be compromised when services are given to off-campus vendors. In "Outsourcing of Technology in Higher Education: The Brookdale Experience," Thompson and Morgovsky (1996) describe the process by which Brookdale Community College in New Jersey utilized the talents and resources of an off-campus vendor to help manage and maintain their technology system. The college hired an outside company, and employees in the college's computing services offices were interviewed to join this independent vendor. Although most employees were offered jobs with comparable benefits and wages, a sense of mistrust and resentment lingered.

Costs of Investing in Technology. Jacobs (1995) also enumerates the fiscal drawbacks of implementing technological tools that require a long-term commitment. He warns that rapid changes in computer technology mean that computers quickly become obsolete, requiring regular upgrades to maintain their usefulness. Keeping current with available software versions is also expensive. Despite the costs, investment in technology has nonetheless become the imperative for community colleges, because "the cost of not renewing technology, of not staying in the mainstream, is that students and faculty will simply stop using it" (p. 37).

Conclusion

Successful implementation of state-of-the-art technologies requires the commitment of community college administrators and an openness to change that may reshape organizational culture. Appropriate funding and the careful allocation of resources are critical to the process. Educational opportunities for faculty, administrators, and staff can help them adapt to new methods of teaching, learning, and information sharing. As part of strategic planning, college administrators should consider developing a position for a full-time information specialist who would be responsible for the installation and maintenance of software and hardware acquired for the college's computer infrastructure. In addition, administrators should ensure that buildings and classrooms provide the necessary space required for the installation of computers and equipment.

Embracing the challenge of technology will ensure that community colleges continue to attract students and prepare them for the twenty-first century. Finally, faculty and staff who work in community colleges should be willing to become proficient in the use of new technologies that enhance the college's academic and administrative services. Ultimately, college communities must recognize and accept the potential for positive change that may alter some of the traditional forms of postsecondary education but that nonetheless will enable higher education to lead our communities into the future.

Note

1. Most ERIC documents (publications with ED numbers) can be viewed on microfiche at approximately nine hundred libraries worldwide. In addition, most may be ordered on microfiche or on paper from the ERIC Document Reproduction Service (EDRS) at (800) 443-ERIC. References preceded by an asterisk (*) refer to journal articles that are not available from EDRS. Journal articles may be acquired through regular library channels or purchased from the following article reproduction services: Carl Uncover: http://www.carl.org/uncover/, uncover@carl.org, (800) 787-7979; UMI: orders@infostore.com, (800) 284-0360; or ISI: tga@isinet.com, (800) 523-1850.

References

Applebaum, C., and others. "Business Process Reengineering: A Consortium Approach with End Users as the Architect Produces Dramatic Results." Paper presented at the Annual CAUSE Conference, New Orleans, La., Nov.–Dec. 1995.

Baltzer, J. A. *The Learning Action Plan: A New Approach to Information Technology Planning in the Community College.* Boulder, Colo.: League for Innovation in the Community College and CAUSE, 1994. (ED 372 803)

*Biehle, J. "What Are the Urgent Design Projects?" *Planning for Higher Education,* 1996, *24* (4), 23–26.

*Brumbaugh, K. E., and McRae, M. S. "An Internet Primer for Community College Administrators." *Community College Journal of Research and Practice,* 1995, *19* (1), 1–11.

Eaton, G., and Grant, R. "Customer Service at Portland Community College—Then and Now." Paper presented at the Annual CAUSE Conference, San Francisco, Dec. 1996.

*Gilbert, S. W. "Educational Technology and Transformation." *Community College Journal,* 1995, *66* (2), 14–18.

*Gilbert, S. W. "Making the Most of a Slow Revolution." *Change,* 1996, *28* (2), 10–23.

*Jacobs, A. "The Costs of Computer Technology." *Community College Journal,* 1995, *66* (2), 34–37.

Johnson, L., and Lobello, S. T. (eds.). *The Twenty-First Century Community College: Technology and the New Learning Paradigm.* Mission Viejo, Calif.: League for Innovation in the Community College, 1996.

LeDuc, A. L. "Personnel Development: Key to Organizational Strength." Paper presented at the Annual CAUSE Conference, San Francisco, Dec. 1996.

*McCabe, R. H. "Beyond the Mirror: Reflecting on Who We Are and Where We Need to Be." *Community College Journal,* 1996, *66* (5), 24–31.

Mellow, G. O. "The Role of the Community College Chair in Organizational Change: Chaos, Leadership and the Challenge of Complexity." Paper presented at the Annual Mid-Atlantic Community College Chair/Dean Conference, Blue Bell, Pa., Oct. 1996. (ED 401 970)

O'Banion, T. (ed). *A Learning College for the Twenty-First Century.* Annapolis Junction, Md.: Community College Press, 1997. (ED 409 042)

Olson, M. A., Muyskens, L., and Busby, N. C. "Attitudes of Community College Faculty and Students Toward the Use of Videodisc Technology in the Classroom." *Community College Journal of Research and Practice,* 1995, *19* (6), 517–528.

Paine, N. "The Role of the Community College in the Age of the Internet." *Community College Journal,* 1996, *67* (1), 33–37. (EJ 528 131)

Reed, C. "The Silicon Ceiling: Technology, Literacy and the Community College Student." Paper presented at the annual meeting of the Conference on College Composition and Communication, Milwaukee, Wis., Mar. 1996. (ED 399 547)

Schroeder, J., and Bleed, R. "Apollo: Changing the Way We Work." Paper presented at the Annual CAUSE Conference, San Francisco, Dec. 1996. (ED 400 899)

Thompson, D., and Morgovsky, J. "Outsourcing of Technology in Higher Education: The Brookdale Experience." Paper presented at the League for Innovation in the Community College's Conference on Information Technology, Phoenix, Ariz., Nov. 1996. (ED 402 974)

JANEL ANN SOULÉ HENRIKSEN is executive assistant to the chief information officer in the Department of Information Technology Systems and Services at Stanford University.

INDEX

ORDERING INFORMATION

NEW DIRECTIONS FOR COMMUNITY COLLEGES is a series of paperback books that provides expert assistance to help community colleges meet the challenges of their distinctive and expanding educational mission. Books in the series are published quarterly in Spring, Summer, Fall, and Winter and are available for purchase by subscription and individually.

SUBSCRIPTIONS cost $55.00 for individuals (a savings of 37 percent over single-copy prices) and $98.00 for institutions, agencies, and libraries. Please do not send institutional checks for personal subscriptions. Standing orders are accepted. Prices subject to change. (For subscriptions outside of North America, add $7.00 for shipping via surface mail or $25.00 for air mail. Orders must be prepaid in U.S. dollars by check drawn on a U.S. bank or charged to VISA, MasterCard, or American Express.)

SINGLE COPIES cost $22.00 plus shipping (see below) when payment accompanies order. California, New Jersey, New York, and Washington, D.C., residents please include appropriate sales tax. Canadian residents add GST and any local taxes. Billed orders will be charged shipping and handling. No billed shipments to post office boxes. (Orders from outside North America must be prepaid in U.S. dollars by check drawn on a U.S. bank or charged to VISA, MasterCard, or American Express.)

SHIPPING (SINGLE COPIES ONLY): $30.00 and under, add $5.50; to $50.00, add $6.50; to $75.00, add $7.50; to $100.00, add $9.00; to $150.00, add $10.00.

DISCOUNTS for quantity orders are available. Please write to the address below for information.

ALL ORDERS must include either the name of an individual or an official purchase order number. Please submit your order as follows:
Subscriptions: specify series and year subscription is to begin
Single copies: include individual title code (such as CC82)

MAIL ORDERS TO:
Jossey-Bass Publishers
350 Sansome Street
San Francisco, California 94104-1342

PHONE subscription or single-copy orders toll-free at (888) 378-2537 or at (415) 433-1767 (toll call).

FAX orders toll-free to (800) 605-2665.

FOR SUBSCRIPTION SALES OUTSIDE OF THE UNITED STATES, contact any international subscription agency or Jossey-Bass directly.